Harriet Hankla
4/30/1915 – 7/22/2004

"Well done, good and faithful servant; you were faithful over a few things ... Enter into the joy of your lord."
Matthew 25:21

Step Out Into the Sunshine

by Harriet Hankla

2020

Copyright © 2020
Tribute Publishing, LLC
Frisco, Texas

Tribute Publishing, LLC

Step Out Into the Sunshine
First Edition September 2020

All Worldwide Rights Reserved
ISBN   978-1-7337727-4-7

All Rights Reserved. No part of this book may be reproduced, stored in a retrieval system, or transmitted, in any form, or by any means, electronic, mechanical, recorded, photocopied, or otherwise, without the prior written permission of the copyright owner or the Author, except by a reviewer who may quote brief passages in a review.

Printed in the United States of America

In God We Trust

Introduction

This is the story of Harriet Hankla. It was her dream to publish her life story in a book.

Harriet's life is a testament to the goodness of God. It is truly a message of hope to all who struggle. She wanted others to know that salvation and peace can be found when we step into the light (sunshine) that only Jesus Christ can offer. For her story, Harriet wanted the words she spoke into her tape recorder many years ago to be written down and published. Tim Malmer, her grandson, listened to her recordings, and through countless hours, transcribed her story word-for-word. The result is what has now become the creation of this book.

By design, the grammar and words were written as Harriet spoke. Some of the recordings were from Harriet talking to groups of people; others were of her recording herself. They have not been modified to meet proper standards; therefore, her words might not be what you are used to reading. If you were fortunate enough to know Harriet, you can hear her voice through the texts of this book as it is written.

Prologue

October 1, 1997

When the Lord tells me anything, I always want to obey and do what he tells me to do as I have told everybody for many years, if the Lord tells you to go out in the street and stand on your head, then you better do it. 'Cause if you don't, He'll get you.

It's been about one month ago, the Lord impressed on me to ask Ken if I could share on some Sunday's. Yet, I didn't want to horn in on his Sermon, but that's what the Lord told me to do...to ask him if I could share my life story. The Lord told me there's not much time. What He meant about that is I don't know. Is it the Lord is coming soon or if I didn't have much time? Whichever way He meant, it's alright. He's in control. But I didn't have much time.

I was in church a couple, three weeks ago. I was so tied up. I felt like I had wires or ropes around me and couldn't much move. I wanted to be free. I didn't want to be tied up with all this down...down. Carol was sitting by me on the floor and I was talking to her and telling her I was so bound up; I must be free. The Lord told me to say that I had broken out of that fence like that horse. The horse was in this fence and he wanted to get out and run and roll in the dust and just be free. And he couldn't get off this fence. It seemed like everything that everyone said that day was being bound down, walls being down, and fences being broken down and all this stuff...just everything was supposed to be broken down. That's the way this whole service went. I felt like I wanted to come out of it and be free. I just didn't want to be bound down like that. The Lord just all-of-a-sudden loosed me. The wires and everything; whatever was tying me down, just fell off of me. I told Debbie, I'm ready to run; I'm free, I'm ready to run. ...just want to get up then and run as hard as I could run. I just wanted to be like that horse out of that fence. I just wanted to get out there and roll in the dust or whatever the Lord wanted me to do. I said that wherever the Lord wanted me to go or whatever He wanted me to do I was going to do it. I just felt so free. I felt like I couldn't stand it, so I got going to do what He wanted me to do. I said that maybe He would take me into a new realm in my life. Maybe it was something that whatever He wanted to do was a new direction. So, after I said that, why Carol was setting down there praying that I would be loosed. The Lord did loose me.

After the service Terry and Debbie came to me and asked if they could have me over to share. And I know that was the Lord. It had to be the Lord. Here, I was wanting to share in Church, but the Lord didn't want me to do that. He didn't want me to take up that time there, but He wanted me to share someplace. I felt like it was just the Lord. So I said, "Well, Lord wherever you want me to go, whatever you want me to say, I'll do it. It don't make any difference how I feel." Today I haven't felt very good at all, I feel so weak but then I know that the ole devil he's right there ready to put whatever on me to keep me from coming over here, but he's fooled because I would have come even If I couldn't walk. If someone had to carry me, I would have come. That's what I want to do. I want to do what the Lord wanted me to do.

The Lord gave me this scripture. In Psalm 19:14, "Let the words of my mouth, and the meditation of my heart, be acceptable in thy sight, O Lord, my strength, and my redeemer." So, I know He's my strength, He's my refuge and a very present help in a time of need. I really need Him now. He's my all in all. He's my everything to me, so I want to obey Him and listen to Him and hear everything He has for me to hear.

So, this story of my life is not gonna be very exciting. Well, I don't know, it might be exciting. It's not going to thrill you too much. Just hang in there because the best is yet to come. As it goes on from Chapter One to Chapter Five, it gets better all the time.

Table of Contents

Introduction i

Prologue iii

Chapter One 1

Chapter Two 19

Chapter Three 37

Chapter Four 53

Chapter Five 75

Chapter Six 95

Chapter One

October 1, 1997

I was born April 30, 1915, Harriet Mandy Ellen Follis. I was born on the Illinois River right on the water in a houseboat. I guess you have all seen a houseboat and you know what that's like. Maybe years ago, it was not as modern as it is now. It was just one room. ...One big room. Bedroom, kitchen, living room was all together. I remember it had four big windows, two on each side. There were two doors, one in the front and one in the back. But anyway, they had the boat tied up and that's where I was born. I remember as far back as three years old. Some people can remember earlier than that, but I don't. When I was three years old, I remember they had this big board and they called it a plank. It went from the boat to the bank. I was going down that plank and fell in the river in four feet of water. I guess I nearly drowned, but I don't remember anything about that, but I do remember falling in. I'm scared to death of the water. I was just three years old and I can remember that. My dad *(Loyd Follis)* lit the lights along the river, each side of the river. He'd go up one side of the river twenty miles and back down twenty miles. He'd light these lights on the river for the purpose of the steamboats, so they knew where they were when they came to these lights. I lived about three miles from this little town that was about five hundred (Hardin, Ill). I don't know if it was that many or not, but it was a very

Chapter One

small town. That's where the steamboats would stop along the way. That's how we would get groceries. We'd get flour, beans and different things like that …coffee and crackers. I remember we'd get crackers in a tin box about this big around *(holding hands about twelve inches apart)*. That was a real treat for us to get a cracker. The boat would stop and let us unload whatever we ordered. We ordered about every three months. There would be a hundred pounds of flour and big boxes of coffee and things that you couldn't buy at a little store. He would light his lights so the steamboat would come in and know where they were and could anchor the steamboat. These lights were run by carbide. It wasn't oil in them or gas, it was carbide. I could smell that stuff today. It just smelled horrible. It smells like tar that you put on the roads. Smells something like that. I can smell it today, them ole carbide lights. We didn't have any transportation. My dad made a sled and put a tub on it. He put us kids in the tub or what would fit in there. There was four of us. The little one especially he put in the tub and put a blanket down in there. He would put on skates and skate down to the neighbors about a mile away. So that's the only transportation we had and only a motorboat. We had a motorboat, but he would go to town or different places. I'd usually hang onto the back of the tub and scoot my feet on the ice because the river would freeze over real thick. My dad could skate all the way to the neighbors. That was our joy ride.

My dad shelled. Most of you don't know one thing about what I mean when I say he shelled. This wasn't in the Illinois River *(holding a sample shell)*. This shell would be like this only

Chapter One

it would have a top to it. He would take hooks on his boat and go out into the middle of the river. They were great big hooks. He would put them hooks down in the bottom of the river and catch these shells. When he felt he had enough on the hooks he'd bring them up and empty them in the boat. They were like clams. Sort of like this *(holding large muscle shell)*. They had a top on them clams muscle meat and muscle shells and all kinds of shells…all kinds of shells small and big. He would get a boat full of shells and would bring them into the bank. They had a great big long vat that they heated water. He got the water boiling. They would put these shells into the hot water to cook them. They would open up when they were heated good. They would take that muscle meat out of them. They put that meat in one pile over here and my mother done this many, many times and that was her job. Taking and cooking these muscles out. Then she'd make a big pile of shells after they got the meat out. Then my dad would take a day off from shellin'. He'd put these shells back in the boat and take these shells twenty miles up the river to a button factory. That's what they made buttons with. That's what buttons was made out of. They don't make them now, they're plastic.

Chapter One

These are all shells *(holding her button collection)*. They would be different colors. Some would be pink some would be blue. He would take these to the button factory and unload them. I don't know how much they got for them. Probably not very much. I imagine if he got $5 for them it would be a big amount. One day my mother and dad was taking these muscles out of these shells and he found a pearl in one of these shells. He sold it for $60. They thought they was rich. I don't know what they got with it. I was too little to remember anything like that. He was so proud that he got that pearl out of that shell. Then every time they picked up a shell, they'd really look to make sure there was any pearls in it.

I had a doll. He might have bought that doll with some of that money. Probably did because he didn't have any money otherwise. I had one doll in my life. It was a china head. I fell and broke the head. I just cried and cried. My doll was broken. My dad had a… he called it the shop where he did a lot of things. I took my doll out to the shop and I said… I always called him Pop… and I said, "Pop, I broke my doll and I want him to fix it." He said, "Well babe, I can't fix it with what I've got." He had solder and he said I can't do it with that so I couldn't get my doll fixed. I cried all the time and I think my mom *(Beulah Alice Mae Peters)* put a rag head…made a head full of rags and put on that doll, but I carried her around for I don't know how long. I was so proud of that doll. She made me rag dolls. I had a lot of rag dolls but that was the nicest doll I ever had. I thought he ought to fix it with what he had. We didn't know what glue was, there wasn't anything like glue.

Chapter One

Then we had a neighbor that had a tent. Eventually I'd go back there a little bit after we... I guess I was about four we pulled the boat out on the bank. We had this neighbor that had a tent. One of our ole hens would go over and lay an egg on his bed every day. That was my job. I would go over there and get that egg every day. I thought that was some great big thing. Every time I'd hear her cackle I'd head for that tent and he'd let me go in there and get the egg. Then one day when I was about five years old, my sister was eight (*Rosalie*), my dad was real sick. Of course, back then no one ever said what was wrong with him. I know he was real sick and real weak. We were supposed to go to the neighbors and get milk for him every day. It was about a half mile or so. We'd go get milk for my dad. One day she gave us a piece of pumpkin pie for him. So, we just kept nibbling on that pie just a little bit. We just wanted to see what it tasted like. So, when we got home it was about maybe a piece that big *(holding fingers the size of a quarter)*. He didn't say anything to us, but we just could not leave that pie alone. Then one day it wasn't too long before he died. I remember I was five. We were out in the yard playing. My little sister was about one year old (*Lillian Marie*) and my brother was about two and a half (*Floyd*). I was chopping wood. I picked up that big ole axe you know and boy I was chopping wood. He was laying in his bed right by the window where he could see out and was kinda watching us. He called me Mandy most of the time. He said, "Mandy you put that axe down, your gonna hurt yourself or one of the little ones." I'd put it down. I just put it down every time he told me to but pretty soon why I didn't think he was looking; I'd pick it up again. I was chopping wood and the axe was really sharp. So pretty soon

Chapter One

he'd holler out the window and say, "Mandy, you put that axe down!" He wasn't a person that would tell you a second time. If he told you once that was it. Then the second time he'd yell, why that was it too. He told me again and I put it down. The next time I picked it up again. Three times I picked that axe up. He didn't say a word. He just came out the door and just could hardly walk. He was so weak and sick. So, he started after me and so I ran way out in the field. He came after me just a little bit. He couldn't walk or run or anything. I ran like a deer. My mother had to come and practically carry him back to the bed. He told her "When she comes in, I want you to go out and get a little elm switch." (They'd really cut you.) "Bring her up to the bed. She disobeyed me and I'll have to whip her." Well when I came in, I didn't have sense enough to know, I guess I wasn't old enough to know that's what he would do. I went in the house and my mother, she had a little switch and she took me up to the bed. He told me "Now babe, I'm gonna have to whip you. You disobeyed me, it wasn't that you ran from me, that was enough you know," but he said, "you disobeyed me. I'm gonna have to punish you." He took that switch, it wasn't that long, but it was keen as it could be. …about as big as my finger. He cut the blood out of my leg. Oh, my land it hurt something terrible. Back then they thought that was you know, they didn't think about abusing you or cutting you or letting the blood run or anything like that. That was the way they punished you. I tell you, I never ran anymore. That was the last time I ever ran from him. My oldest son did the same thing with me. I did the same thing to him and he never ran from me either. That was the first and the only whippin' my dad ever gave me. Of course, he died not long

Chapter One

after that he had gotten so sick and there wasn't any doctor. There was this old doctor that came to the house to see how you were doing. They just didn't call the doctor every time you turned around. He got so sick that he had to be moved someplace where he could get some care. No hospitals, no daycare, no nursing homes or anything like that. We never heard of it. They had a place called the poor farm. Well I tell you that was a good name for it 'cause it was for people that was homeless and couldn't take care of themselves or anything. They put him in this room that was screen all around. This was in the fall of the year. We stayed in a building that everybody else stayed in. They gave us spoiled beans for breakfast. My mother was put out with that. She said if you'll just let me… there was a house with a couple of rooms. If you'll just do this, I mean just give us this house and I'll bring some food and I'll feed my kids 'cause I don't want you to feed them spoiled beans. So that's what they did they gave us that house. I guess they must have moved furniture or something from out of the houseboat. My dad was in this one room.

Thanksgiving Day, my dad wanted chicken and dumplings. He called them pants patches. They were just squares cut square. My mother killed one of the hens we had and made him some dumplings, pants patches. They weren't done yet and she heard him calling for her and she went to see about him and when she got there he was gone. So, he didn't get to have Thanksgiving dinner or his pants patches. Then after he died, that was the first time I was ever in church. I don't remember even too much about it. We went to the funeral. We went in a team of horses and a wagon. I think that was

Chapter One

the way they even hauled him to the cemetery. So, then we buried him up on a hill at this cemetery they had *(Humphrey Cemetery Bee Creek Rd. 26 miles from Hardin).*

Then we moved in with my grandmother and grandpa *(Robert W Peters and Harriet Mandy Ellen Lynn).* We stayed there a year. Well they lived in a one room house, and they had my two uncles *(Ernest Lee and Elba Lamont Peters),* four of us kids, and my mother. There was about seven or eight of us...all in that one room. I can see today just where everything was placed. The bedroom was in the end of the house and the living room was in the middle. My grandmother had a real old...I don't know, they didn't call them couches or anything, but anyway it was real old with a round back and in the kitchen she had an old wood stove. She'd make them ole thick biscuits out of baking soda and sourdough. We ate good. Didn't have much money, but she always raised everything she had. My grandpa worked out clearing land or doing whatever he could for other people. He died while we was living with him with grandma and grandpa. He was not very old either. My dad was 27 years old *(Correction: 31)* when he died left four children. Before he died, my grandpa, he had a beautiful apple tree about this high *(four feet).* He'd just prune that thing and take care of it and fertilize it and do everything. It was a real nice young apple tree. So, one day I took a notion to get the hatchet and I cut it down. I don't even remember doin' it, but I remember getting the hatchet and I remember cutting it down, but I didn't remember much about doin' it. So, when he came home why grandma told him about it. I was out playing, so he came out and told me to come to him. I knew what was coming. He said,

Chapter One

"Mandy did you cut my apple tree down?" I said, "Yes." I didn't lie to him, I just, I couldn't lie. I had to tell him I did it and he knew I did it. He said, "Well, you shouldn't have done it, it was my prized tree. It was just really a nice young tree, a special apple." I told him well, I cut it down. He took me by the heels...my feet...took hold of my feet and put me down in the cistern head first. I thought I was gonna die. Oh, my goodness, that was the awfullest thing for anyone to do and I couldn't understand why he would do anything like that. And there again there was water in the cistern. A cistern is something that the rainwater runs in. Sometimes we drank it, but mostly it was for worshing clothes and your hair and stuff like that. But anyway, that cistern had a lot of water in it. He put me in there, I don't know how long it was probably two or three minutes, but it seemed like a week to me. I was so scared I think I just ran and hid someplace. He told me well that's the way I'm gonna punish you for cutting my tree down. I never cut another tree. I don't know about this cutting. Today I can't cut anything. I was always cutting down something. Anyway, I got through that. He didn't whip me, but I would rather gotten a whippin' with a switch than I would to be put down in the cistern.

We had to carry water from the spring way down under the hill to use for drinking water and cooking water and such. I remember there was one time that while I lived at grandma and grandpa's they decided that the kids were... well my uncles were like 17 or 18 and my oldest sister, she was about 8 and I was 5 ...and they thought they could leave us long enough to go to town. They went to get groceries one day ...left us all there by ourselves. I guess they thought my

Chapter One

uncles was old enough to baby sit for us. Me and my sister and brother and my little sister, I don't remember if she was in on it too *(Rosalie, Mandy, Floyd and Lillian Marie)*, but we all had got into the bottom of the cabinet and got coffee. She had coffee beans and every morning grandma would grind coffee beans fresh. We got in that coffee can and ate coffee until we were drunker than an ole…we was really drunk. All that caffeine…so anyway we ate coffee 'till we couldn't eat anymore. We was so drunk we didn't even know what we was doing. They came home and they wondered what in the world was wrong with us kids. We was just acting pretty strange. Finally, somehow or another we had mind enough to tell them what we did. Maybe the coffee can was sitting out there about empty. Anyway, they knew what had happened. We'd about ate all the coffee beans. I don't remember getting any punishment for that, I just don't remember.

About a year we stayed with grandma and grandpa, then we moved the houseboat out along the bluff. When I was born on the river, they always said I was a "river rat." When I moved out on the bluff, they called me a "hillbilly." When they moved this boat out along the road along the bluff, they called me a hillbilly. I said I didn't care what they called me. My mother always said that we were bachelors. It was just her and us four kids. We made the best of it. Grandma and Grandpa gave us a cow and gave us chickens for eggs. She made butter and sold eggs to make a living. That's all the money she ever had making butter and eggs.

Chapter One

I remember we didn't go to church 'cause my mother wouldn't let us go to church because we didn't have clothes good enough. She always made all of our clothes and she just didn't think we had clothes good enough to go to church. It was about 3 miles to town and it's where I had to walk to school. I had one dress in September when school started. I wore it all winter until spring. I'd come home and wash it out and starch it and get ready for the next day. Anyway, we didn't go to church but every Sunday my mother would have us to clean up the house real good and have it shining. She didn't have any rugs or linoleum or anything. It was just the bare old floor. We would clean the house all up good and whenever we got through, she would sit in the rocking chair. My sister would sit on one rocker and I would be on the other one. Or my brother would be on the rocker and I'd stand on the rockers in the back. That was a load on that ole rocker. It must have been a good one. We'd sing songs like "Bringing in the Sheaves" and something about a soldier volunteer and "Joy Bells ringing in your Heart" and "Leaning on the Everlasting Arms." We would just sing all them songs that she knew. She had the family Bible, but she never read out of the Bible. We had another book that someone came along peddling these books and she bought one of these books and it had a lot of pictures in it that told about the birth of Jesus.

She'd read that to us. I never heard her pray when I was a kid. I know she must have prayed. I think she had the idea that she had to be quiet to herself and not pray out loud. I don't know it to be, so I just took it as that's the way it was. But anyway, I never heard her pray until after I got older.

Chapter One

Anyway, that's how we had our Sunday service. We had to have the house cleaned up before. We had this cow that my grandma and grandpa had given us. Every Sunday we went to grandmas. Sometimes it would be dark when we'd get home. She'd take this cow and put it on a big chain and tie it out where it could get grass. She took this cow that morning down...we called it the bottom...pretty close to where we were. It was late when we got home. I always went with her to get the cow and help her milk. A great big owl, a hoot owl came down and flogged us. Just pulled our hair out and scratched us all over. My mother was just scratched. They have just terrible sharp feet. They just about tore us up. She took this chain when it got lose...this great big ole log chain and beat it to death. She killed it with this chain. Things like this I remember. I might not remember everything.

She always had a garden where she raised all her food. Nearly just like coffee and flour and stuff like that. We'd pick blackberries and strawberries. Anything that was edible we'd pick, and she'd can them and make jelly and all this kinda stuff.

Up on the hill was an orchard. This owner of the orchard said this one tree was hers and she could just have it all. So, we'd go up on that hill and get these apples and she'd make apple butter, apple pie, apple preserves, apple jelly, everything she could do with apples. She'd peel the apples to make apple butter. She would take these peelings and worsh them good and everything and put 'em on and boil them and that's what she would make the jelly out of. That

Chapter One

was the best part 'cause that is where it's got all the good stuff in them peelings. She'd make jelly and all kinds. Blackberry jelly, wild strawberry not very big, but anyway she would make something out of them. One day we went to pick blackberries. This one guy that owned the land there told her that this patch of blackberries is yours. Pick all you want, and he wouldn't let anyone else in there...great big blackberries. So, we took our buckets and picked blackberries and had our buckets full. About that time, he come along and said you're not supposed to be in there. He was just teasing. He was just tormenting her. She said I thought you told me I could pick berries all I wanted. He said No, I never told you that. He was just really giving her a hard time. Pretty soon she just had enough of it. She took one of them buckets and threw it right in his face and said, "Here are your berries if you want them that bad." Then we never picked berries there anymore. That was terrible, pickin' in the hot sun and everything. Well that was one little incident that happened while we were bachelors. She would pick wild greens. Probably none of you know what that is. You can go out to the woods and there is a lot of different kind of greens that I'd give anything in the world if I could get out there and pick some now. She'd bring them home and mix them all up. She knew every kind that was good to eat. She'd take them home and worsh them and worsh them. We had to carry water for I don't know how long. We had to carry water to worsh them and worsh them. She would worsh them through three or four waters and get 'em clean. She'd put a big piece of fat meat in them. We would eat the big fat meat too. I can see her with that old tined fork. After they cooked for a while she'd dip in with that fork. I can see

Chapter One

her today. She would get that fork and taste them to see if they were seasoned right and to see if they were done. She had a big ole iron pot on a wood stove cooking. Oh, they were good. They tasted so good. Anyway, that was one of the things. Then after we got to going to school, she baked her own bread. About 4 pm we'd get home and she'd just take that bread out of the oven. Big ole loaves about that long *(12 inches)*. She said she didn't like to cut hot bread and she just broke it up 'cause…I don't know she had all kinds of superstitious things if you cut hot bread it was bad luck and all this kind of stuff. She'd just break it and put it on the table and set us down with butter and Karo syrup and that's what we would eat. I can almost taste it now. We'd be so hungry when we come home from school. Not every night 'cause she'd only bake bread 'bout three times per week. Anyway, it was sure good. I remember I was always kind of a tomboy really. I was running through the house and she had that oven door down and it was as hot as it could be. I ran past there, and I burned my legs. It was real bad. I got the scar yet today from that burn on my leg. We had such a wonderful time. It was such a peaceful life. So peaceful, so contented although we didn't have anything; no furniture, fine clothes, money or nothing. We were just really happy. I remember them days so well it was just really a good time in my life.

I went to school. I had to walk to school about three miles. In the wintertime the snow would be that deep *(four feet)* and cold, it was so cold. We had to walk to school, three miles to school and three miles back. One morning we was kinda late and, oh we was hurrying and the snow was so deep that

Chapter One

we couldn't even walk hardly. My mother would take grass sacks and wrap 'em around on our legs and feet to keep them warm and dry as we could. We didn't know what a boot was or an overshoe or anything, so she just wrapped them sacks around 'em. We was pluggin' through that deep snow, we couldn't hardly hurry because you couldn't walk in them and of course little kids about this high you couldn't walk very good. This old guy who lived down lower, he came along in his new car. He had a Model A or a Model T whichever was first. He came along in that car and boy it was just shining like a pewter nickel and he stopped. I remember his name was Bossom *(or Bussen)*. He always smoked a cigar. Mr. Bossom came along and passed us a bit and stopped. We thought he was gonna give us a ride. We hurried up as fast as we could, and we got in. Pretty soon he looked back and said, "What are you kids doing in here?" I said, 'Well I thought you was givin' us a ride." He said, "Well, I just stopped to light my cigar." So, I told my brother let's get out. We started gettin' out. My brother was out, and I was almost out when he said, "Well, since you're in here, well get back in and I'll take you the rest of the way." It liked to scared us to death because we thought we were doing something wrong and that's why we thought he stopped.

Then one day when I was goin' to school I'd go on a picnic all by myself. I'd grab a cold biscuit, an onion and a tomato if it happened to be in the summertime and I went on a picnic all by myself. I'd went across over by the creek over by this big ole tree and I'd have me a picnic. Oh, it tasted so great. Lot of times when we'd go to school, why we didn't have anything hardly to take in our lunch, so mom would put

Chapter One

in some sorghum molasses. It turns black especially on a biscuit and that's what we'd take to school for our lunch. I was ashamed at my lunch and I'd get way over behind a tree or someplace to eat my lunch 'cause I didn't want somebody to see what I had for my lunch. These other kids would have sandwiches or different things you know, and peanut butter and jelly was almost…well, jelly, but peanut butter …we never had peanut butter, but if they did have it, you know, they was rich. We never heard of it. Well I didn't want them to see my biscuit and Sorghum molasses because it would turn that ole biscuit just as black as it could be. Well one day mom got enough money ahead she gave us a nickel to buy us a little can of potted meat. So, we went to the store and we wasn't supposed to go off to school then, but she gave us permission to go off to the store and get that potted meat and boy we thought we was rich as anybody. It tasted better on that biscuit than that other. Then we would go off to school. There were trees along the road that was called paw paws something like a banana, but they are shorter than a banana. They have great big ole seeds in them. We'd eat them and they tasted really better than a banana.

I'd play jacks and jump rope. That's the only thing that we knew back then. We had measles, mumps, whooping cough and all this kind of stuff which every kid has, but I had the mumps and I tell you, I was swollen out here like this, but I wanted pickles. Mom said "You can't have pickles. That's the worst thing you can eat." I just kept telling her I wanted pickles. That's what I had a taste for, so she went to the cellar and said "I only got one jar of pickles left." She didn't want to give them to me because they say there really hard

Chapter One

on you when you eat something sour like that. Yet today, I can just look at something sour and it's like my jaw is about to come off. So, she got them pickles and gave them to me and I remember how good they tasted. She had all of her own remedies...home remedies. They would kill this skunk and she would render the oil out of this skunk and put in the oven and cook it to render it out. She would mix it and use it by itself, called skunk oil. She'd rub it all over our chests, our backs and palms of our hands and feet and everything and boy it would knock the cold. It was a real good remedy. Then she'd take turpentine and lard and rub us good with that when we had a cold *(Also known as a Coal Oil Rag or Sally Rag)*. Then she made up an acifidity bag. She'd put it in a little bag and tie it around our neck *(Resin of the root of the* **Asafetida** *plant)*. That was supposed to keep all the germs away. Now where acifidity came from I don't know. I still don't know today where it came from. She'd mix it up some way or another and put it in a little ball like and sew it up in a little bag and put it around our necks. Kids didn't even want to get around me. It would stink to high heaven. I tell you it was the stickiest stuff I ever smelt in my life.

This is about the end of this part of my story. It's chapter one. This might not have been very exciting to you. But when I think about looking back and seeing my life, it's kinda exciting to me.

Chapter One

Chapter Two

October 8, 1997

I just wanted to pick up a few things where I left off the other day. One thing I wanted to tell you is that I missed a lot of school. I had to take the 5th grade and the 7th grade over twice. I lost a lot of school years because I was sick. I had so much sickness that I just wasn't able to go to school. The one thing that we had was diphtheria. They was several…I don't know how many the kids in school that died with it. It was just really bad. I didn't get to go to school that one whole season. The school year I didn't go at all. I remember when we were sick, the whole family was sick. Even my mother took diphtheria…and my sister, she had what they called the black diphtheria. Her tong turned just as black as it could be. She was paralyzed after she had it. We carried her around. Me and my brother would make a seat and carry her around like that for a long time. I don't remember how long, but it was a long time before she could ever walk. But anyway, all of us had the diphtheria and my mother had it. Then my grandmother came to take care of us then she got it. We were all in the winter getting sick. I remember this priest that was in town, we lived about three miles south of town. This priest would bring us half gallon of milk every morning just as sure as the morning would come by, he'd bring that half gallon of milk. Father Daley was his name. He was so good to us. He'd just set it right on the door or

Chapter Two

right inside the porch and we'd know that he left it, but he wouldn't come in 'cause you know it was a very contagious disease. The town, around Christmastime, they brought us candy and nuts and shoehorns, and my mother had just gotten a #3 worsh tub. We just put all of that candy and nuts and everything all in that tub. They're pretty big. We had candy for so long, but my mother wouldn't let us eat only just a little bit at a time. Each day she'd let us eat just a little bit not just to save it, but she didn't think it was good for us to eat too much candy, which is right. But anyway, I remember that tub being full of candy. I think there was a few oranges, but we never got oranges only at Christmastime. We'd get an orange and a little bag of candy from town hall. That's the only time I ever had an orange. Boy I tell you, we'd just eat one little piece of it at a time and save it for the next day. It was so good.

I was 10 when my mother got married again *(to Leonard McGee)*. We were still bachelors. She always called us bachelors 'cause we just took care of ourselves the best that we could. I was 9 or 10 years old. My stepdad was so mean to us. Why he was just really mean. Way back there, they didn't hardly know how to, or I don't think they knew how to raise a child the right way. Well, he hit me over the head with a poker one day. I was such a…I knew I had something coming, but I would sass him back and I'd talk back to him and I'd get the last word in if that was the last thing I done. But I was sassin' him and he hit me over the head. I got ridges on my head today when he did that and just knocked me out. I was out. Then he took a bucket of water and threw it on my face to bring me to and he thought he was

Chapter Two

doing something to correct me or to punish me. But anyway, it was bad. Finally, I got able to get up and go to school. It was really bad. I say it was a wonder my brain works as good as it does 'cause that's a real blow on the head. But anyway, they was several things ...and he would make us work so hard and I was the one that would have to get out in the wintertime and help him saw wood. I'd get on the other end of that big ole crosscut saw. It was just awful hard, and I was so skinny and little. I was just skin and bones. But I had to get out there and help him cut wood and do everything outside like that; fill the wood box and all this kind of stuff. Besides, I had to work in the house and get all of the work done; dishes done, beds made, floors swept and everything before we went to school. That was an everyday thing. We had to do that before we went to school. Sometimes I thought, well my mother didn't do anything. We did all the work and everything. But I'm sure there was a lot of work she had to do after that. But anyway, we just had to work real hard.

One thing that stands out in my mind and I never will understand all about it. I was maybe 14 or 15, I'd go outside of the house and I'd set down by the house. Where this come from, I guess the Lord was dealing with me I don't know, but he had to have something to do with it. But I would just sit down there, and I would just pray and preach... just really was into it you know. I had never gone to church before. I didn't know anything about the Lord. I didn't know about Jesus and I had never heard that word. I don't think I even thought about that there was a higher power. But anyway, the Lord had a purpose in that. I know

Chapter Two

He was in it or I couldn't have done it. But I don't even remember what I said, but I know I was preachin' up a storm. ...and just praying. But I never can get it in my mind just where it came from, but I know it must have come from the Lord.

Later on, when I got about 13 or 14 years old these short skirts came in which I detest today. I would pull my dress up. We'd always have a belt on our dress. We'd pull that dress up and blouse it over past our knees. We wore long underwear in the wintertime and black bloomers. So, I'd go to school and all the other girls, of course, they didn't have to wear long underwear and them big ole heavy stockin's. Mom would make us garters and we'd roll them down to keep 'em up. So, one day I went to school and the girls had their short dresses on and their socks rolled down and that was when they rolled their socks right below the knee. Boy they was just goin' around like they thought they was something. I thought well if them girls can do it then I can too. So I rolled my stockin's down and I had to take these underwear and roll them way up here and then I'd roll my stockin's down below my knee and then I'd take and put my dress up over my belt and bring my dress up. I thought I was just really in style. When I got ready to go home from school, well we walked three miles home and before we come around the corner, my sister says, you better put that dress down and roll them socks back up cause you know what mom will do. I said well, she don't ever pay attention to me. She don't even see me. Well I got fooled. I came home and of course you always change your school clothes and put another old dress on. I went in and changed my

Chapter Two

clothes and I did the same thing. I made it short and rolled my stockin's. My mother didn't say one word. I didn't think she'd even seen me. I was outside, I was a tomboy and I was running and playin' around. So pretty soon, she came around the corner of the house and she had a switch and she just switched me really good for rollin' them stockin's down. She didn't even tell me what she was doin'...I knew, I knew what she was doin' and I never rolled my stockin's anymore, I might have when I was at school, but I'd put 'em back up before I got home. But my sister warned me, that's what it would be like.

Then I'd take them little Cloverine Salve boxes. I don't know if you've ever seen them or not, they still have them around.

I'd take one of them little boxes and put flour in it for face powder and then we had red crape paper that probably we got from the junk hole. We'd take that red crape paper and

Chapter Two

wet it for lipstick, and we'd make rouge you know all around. We'd have our face painted up like an Indian and I'd just go around like I was the richest person in the world. I'd sneak that flour out 'cause if mom would've seen it, why she wouldn't let me have it. I'd go up on the hill and I was just really dressed up you know. I can remember doing that.

Then one day I decided to make me some bangs. I had real long hair come way down like that *(waving hand below knee)*. So I decided the girls at school had bangs, so I wanted some bangs. So, I got the scissors and I went out behind the house and I made me some bangs. Well I got it again for cuttin' my hair, 'cause back then she said that I promised my dad that I wouldn't cut my hair. Well I was so little when he died, I didn't remember anything. Anyway, my sister had never cut her hair in her life. She still had long hair when she died. Anyway, I cut my bangs, and I don't imagine they were very straight. It was a long time before them bangs growed out.

Chapter Two

MOTHER AND DAUGHTER WITH LONG HAIR

Mrs. Leonard McGee, right, and her oldest daughter, Mrs. Everett Kitson, have never had their hair cut. Mrs. McGee's hair measures 59 inches long and Mrs. Kitson's 43 inches. These two ladies are well known residents of Hardin. Some people say long hair is pretty but too much trouble to care for, but Mrs. McGee and Mrs. Kitson seem to enjoy combing and pinning up their tresses. Everyone who knows them will say their hair always looks nice. This picture was taken by Mrs. McGee's other daughter, Mrs. Harriet Hankla of Kankakee. Harriet is very proud of her mother and sister's long hair and thought others should see how long and pretty it is. Mrs. Hankla and husband visited Thanksgiving Day with her mother and family.

Chapter Two

Rosalie Follis-Kitson (Left) with mother Beulah Alice Mae Peters (right). Picture by Harriet Mandy Ellen Follis-Hankla

Then I would take before that, I would take and wet my hair real wet. I'd make waves all in on the side of it so I would have some waves in my hair. I said I guess my hair has been done that way so much all during my growin' up years, I still got kinda a little wave there and I don't have a permanent. I haven't had a permanent in two years, I think. But anyway, that's the way they did, they just made them waves and spit curls. That's what they was called, spit curls, just a little bitty wad of hair down here and then you would curl them over

Chapter Two

you know. I'd make them. She didn't say too much about that but I know she didn't like it, but then I'd just wet that hair so sopping wet to make them waves. I look back and see things that I did 'course I imagine every kid does things like that. So, this was during the depression years. We didn't have…there was no work no food sometimes we just didn't have anything to eat at all. My dad, I remember had worked oh, maybe a week or something like that and the guy didn't pay him and we got to where we just didn't have anything to eat. So he said well I'll think I'll go down there and see if he could pay me my money. What he paid was only about six dollars and somethin'.

But anyway, it was enough, I remember him getting some little stick of bologna and a loaf of bread. We didn't even have flour to make bread at home. So, he got a loaf of bakers bread and boy I tell you that was better than a cake. Times were real hard then, but in June of 1932, I graduated from the 8th grade. I was 17 years old. Because I lost so much schooling that I was just 17 years old when I graduated out of the 8th grade. Well today they don't make such a big to-do over the 8th grade, but then, back then it was a big thing to graduate from the 8th grade. My mother wouldn't let me go to high school because I didn't need any more education to get married and have kids. I tell ya, she was wrong, but 'course I didn't know any better either. But anyway, I graduated from the 8th grade and my mother made me a dress and a hat; big wide brim hat out of flour sacks, and she'd starch it and it would stand up as stiff as it could be. And the dress she made me, the dress out of flour sacks and my sister, she was married, and she had just gotten a new pair of

Chapter Two

white shoes, white shoes…we'd used to call them slippers. It wasn't them big ole button shoes that we used to wear. I thought I was dressed up and they was white. I'm not sure, but I think I had white stockings on. I was always dressed in white. And I went to the graduation and boy I tell you, I was really dressed up the best as you could. I think I looked about as good as the rest of them, they all had new dresses and everything. They had more money than we did and most of their mothers made their clothes. I was really proud of that dress and she made them out of flour sacks.

I graduated on the 4th of June and got married Dec 26th of that same year. But I had to have a home. I didn't have any home at that time, so I got married to keep from worshing dishes *(laughing)*. Well I fooled myself. My husband that I married later on he would haul corn past our house in a flatbed truck. I don't know what you would call it, ear corn or what, but anyway he would haul corn past our house and he'd always wave at me and I didn't dare wave at him. Mom seen me wave at him she'd of come after me again. I didn't. I was always outside and I finally got to where I knew that he would be coming by and I'd get behind the house where there was no windows so that she couldn't see out. He'd wave at me you know… And he went home, and he told his parents he said well I found my wife today. She lives down there along the road and she's got pig tails. I always had. Mom always fixed my hair…well after I got to where I could fix my own hair, comb my own hair, why I did it myself. She always parted it in the middle and had two great big long braids and put a red ribbon on the end of them. So he, that's what he said she's got pig tails and she lives down there along

Chapter Two

the road and that's the woman I'm gonna marry. Neither one of us ever thought about that we'd ever get married, but that's what he determined; that he'd found his wife. Then along, well between the time I graduated along that summer why we took the measles. Back then we had the measles bad they was just oh, you was really sick. My mother, she took the measles and she was pregnant with twins, but she lost the twins. My stepdad told me well, if you'd just do the work, (which I was doing all the work anyway) he says if you take care of mom and do the work then I'll pay ya. Well, I was just all thrilled to do the work and I was gonna get some money. I just did everything and boy I worked so hard to take care of her. About three weeks she was able to get up and take care of herself. So, I told dad I said well you told me if I took care of mom and do the work, you'd pay me. Oh, my land he liked hit the ceiling. He said you set your foot under the table the same as I do, I don't think I owe you anything. I says, well dad you told me that you would pay me. 'Course I got sassin' back and talkin' back to him and he didn't do anything but say, you just go in there and get your belongings, and I remember everything I owned was in one dresser drawer. He says you get them clothes and you leave. Well I was just…Oh it just hurt me awful that he'd make me leave home. My mother never said a word. 'Course I was 17 years old.

I went in there and I got a pillowcase and I put everything in there I owned in that pillowcase and put it across my back, and I walked fifteen miles over the hill. I went to my grandmothers first. Then my sister lived down under in the valley like. So, I went to grandma's and she said well, you

Chapter Two

can't stay here. And that's one of the things I could never understand. I thought well your own grandmother won't let you stay. I never understood that. It was gettin' almost dark, so I had to go down under the hill to get to my sisters. It was fifteen miles all together that I walked over the hill and to my sisters and they lived with her mother-in-law. I knocked on the door and she'd seen who it was, and she invited me in. So, I asked her could I stay, and I told her what happened. She said well we don't have much, but she said if you will help me do the worsh (and we had to carry water from way down under the hill from a spring) she said if you'll just help me do the work, you can stay. So I stayed there 'bout maybe a couple of weeks. My sister was sick with the flu and she had a real small baby. Their first baby. Her mother-in-law said I could take care of her and help with the baby, so that's what I did.

Then my grandmother and two uncles was gonna go about fifty miles to this little country church because my aunt had lived up there and they went to church and they was all saved and the kids saved and my grandmother and two uncles went, and so they wanted me to go. I went with them one day. Well when it comes to Sunday school time why my cousins were a lot smaller than I was a lot younger, they went into the junior class. They wanted me to go into the junior class with them. I thought well, I'm just a big girl, I didn't want to go in that junior class. I want to go in the big girl's class. They just kept wantin' me to go down there. Well who was the teacher, but my husband that I married. If I'd o' had something handy I would have hit him with it. At first thing off he says, "Can you read?" Oh, I just felt like taking

Chapter Two

something and hittin' him over the head. It embarrassed me and everything so much and 'course he knew what he was doin', he was just teasin' me. He asked me if I could read. That just made me kinda mad at him. That same day why, he asked me if he could walk me to my aunt's house. Well they lived up on a big hill and the church was oh, maybe it was a mile away from where my aunt lived. He walked me to my aunt's place. We both fell in love with each other about the same time. He came then down to my sisters to see me. We was sittin' there. We had to set up all night and take care of my sister and give her medicine or something. But anyway, we were settin' up all night with her. We was sittin' on one of these day beds that they used to have. We was lookin' at a catalog that was called a Chicago mail order catalog. Everything I would see in there I'd say, "Oh that sure is pretty, I'd like to have that." Just not even thinkin' what I was sayin'. Everything I'd come to "Oh I'd like that, I wish I had that." So, he was taking notes in his mind all the time what I would say that I liked. There was a hat that I liked and there was a coat and a dress and a pair of shoes. I picked it out, but I didn't have any money to buy anything. I remember though I had made me a dress while I was there and I run the sewing machine through my finger clear down through the nail and I tell you we liked to have a time gettin' that needle out of that nail. I didn't buy any clothes. He went home at about oh, maybe midnight.

One day I got a letter. Well I got this package in the mail and my, that was just a real treat to get anything in the mail. You never got even a letter or anything. So, I got this big package and it had that coat and that dress and that hat and

Chapter Two

shoes all in it. So, I got the letter (he wrote a letter). I got it the same day that I got this package. It says, well the clothes was meant for a Christmas present, but if you would like you can use 'em for wedding garments. If you want to, if you like that, I said "I like" right now! I wanted to use them. I don't even know what color. I know the coat was black with a brown fake fur collar on it. The hat was black, but I can't remember what the dress was like. I think it was some kind of a wine color or burgundy. Wasn't like wedding gowns we have today. I didn't know that they was any difference. I didn't know you had to wear white or anything. It didn't matter to me. They was just clothes to put on. Well anyway, when he came back, I told him that, that was alright with me and that's when I said I got married to have a home and to keep from worshing dishes. But I did love him. I, you know I didn't get married just…. I didn't have any home and I thought well that would be a good way to get a home. So, we got married then on Dec 26th. Three weeks, I think it was about three weeks or a little over three weeks from the time I'd met him 'till we was married. We was married like in three months bein' married 20 years when he died, so that's a, you know just the start of the next chapter. Graduatin' in June and getting' married in December of that same year was kinda….17, 18 years old. Well, I wasn't quite 18. My mother would have had to sign for me. We went to another town and when the ole judge (we's just married by a judge) he asked me how old I was. Well, before I could even think to tell him how old I was why my husband, he said uh, 18. So that's how we got out of that without her havin' to sign for us. Well that was old for people to get married. Usually people got married around 17 or 18. I think my mother was

Chapter Two

maybe 18 or 19. *Audience question: "After you left the house did you talk to your mom?"* Oh yes, I'd go home, and he didn't say anything about it. He'd let me come home. But, he just wouldn't want me to stay home. I was out on my own. As soon as you got 17, 18 years old, you was out. You was on your own. Yeah, I went home fact of the matter, I went home and he asked my mother if he could have me. So, my mother sat there for about 5 minutes and didn't say a word.

Pretty soon she said, well if your Johnny Vetter's boy she says I know that you're alright. You're a good man. She grew up with his dad, so she knew what he was like. So, she says if you're as good a person that your dad was, why it's alright. We was tickled about that. We had to go home to ask her if we could get married. She said yes. He was seven years older than I was. I was 17 and he was 25. It was quite a…you know seven years older than I was. I didn't notice anything, and it didn't matter to me. We just loved each other. I don't think that has anything to do with a marriage. Specially that old, just seven years.

Audience question: "What did his family think about you?" Oh, they was just thrilled to death over me. They just liked me from the very first, and oh yeah they were real good people to me. I couldn't have gotten through life a lot of times if it hadn't been for both of them specially my father-in-law. He was just so good to me and helped me so many times. I would make biscuits and I'd forget to put…I'd just…all I'd put in them was flour and water and when they'd come in to eat lunch why they'd be so hard as bricks you know and my two or three brother-in-laws, they'd just tease me and say well you'd knock a bull down with them. And they just teased me, and he'd stood back after they went back to work why he stayed in and talked to me and said why don't pay attention to any of them boys. They just tease ya, and if they didn't love you, they wouldn't tease ya. He said next time said you go to make bread you just stop and think, *have I got everything in there?* And there's just been several times he's helped me so much and 'course my mother-in-law was just so good to me and helped me so much and I really just thanked the Lord afterwards. They were a Christian family.

That was one of the things I appreciated too after I got to be a Christian myself, that I had Christian in-laws and it was just so wonderful. I had three half-brothers and a sister and a brother. I had two sisters, but one of them died when she was about three. We were real close family. My stepdad kind of gave me a lot of problems. I mean you know he'd give me a lot of trouble. I still loved him, and I'd forgive him. We were a real close family. My sister and I, we was just…I still haven't gotten over it yet and she's been gone about 15 years. She was about 73 I think it was. She was three years older than I was. She had leukemia and died. But we were so close that today a lot of things I want to know about the family, I just want to go to her and ask her. I really miss her more than I do my mother. We were real, real close. I appreciated that. I appreciated the closeness I had with my family. This was the sister that was paralyzed. We've had a lot of rough times in our life. You can't just sit and dwell on the past. It's good that I can remember all of these things down through the years. And that's one thing too I just thank the Lord that my mind is as good as it is. I forget a lot of things, but then

Chapter Two

I don't think there is a one of you here that don't forget, and I do too. Now I can remember way back there, but I can't remember what I had for breakfast. My mind is good and clear, so I thank the Lord for that. I'm so glad, so thankful that I can remember all of that stuff. I imagine there is a lot more I should've gotten in. But didn't figure it was too important. I know so many people today, some old people that has Alzheimer's disease, and I hope I never get that way 'cause nobody wants to get that way. It's just bad when you don't remember anything, you don't know anything you don't know anybody. But my ole brain, my pea brain I've got, it works good. I forget sometimes, but somebody just said that they was this preacher that came to this lady's house that was dyin' and he says well ma'am have you ever thought about the hereafter? She says oh yes, I think about it all the time. I go to the kitchen and I ask myself, what am I here after? And that's the way I do, sometimes I go from one room to the other, and I'll think now what did I come in here for? Like the ole guy was down to the foot of the steps and says well was I goin' up or did I just come down. He couldn't remember.

Chapter Two

Chapter Three

October 15, 1997

My husband to be came and got me on Christmas day and we went to his parent's home and they were putting a hard road through paved road and the road we had to go over to get to his parents; they didn't have it finished. It was real muddy and we'd gotten stuck so we had to leave the car down to the road where we came, where the hard road had been finished. So, we had to walk over a hill about, I don't know how many miles it was, but it was way over a big ole hill. Snow was clear up to your waist. It was just really deep and snow drifts. You'd sink down in the drifts and leaves made it really hard to walk. I had an ole raincoat that was rubber. It was just made out of rubber; it wasn't like the raincoats today. I had a coat on and then I had this raincoat over it. And everything I could get to keep warm; it was just oh my I don't know how cold it was, it was just zero. So, we walked over the hill and got to his house and his mother had a big feast. Chicken and dumplings, I can taste them yet and homemade candy, oh just everything you can imagine she had, and we got there just in time to eat. It was gettin' dark just the time we got there. So, we ate and the next morning, why we got up to get ready to go be married. His sister and her friend had a model T Coupe. I had to sit on my husband-to-be's lap. Just a little bittie ole thing. You couldn't hardly sit four of us in that little bittie one seat. That's the way we

Chapter Three

went over to this other town about ten, fifteen miles to this town to get married. My husband and his brother had been workin' on this hard road. His brother had a check of $21 and his check was only $9. I don't know why, but he didn't work as much or something. So, they traded checks so $21 is what we had to get married on. I don't know how much it was, what they charged to marry us. We got married by the judge. The justice of the peace. We had to borrow a ring 'cause he didn't have a ring. He didn't have money enough for a ring. We borrowed his aunts ring. Well we got over there and the ole judge asked or wanted to know how old I was, before I could even get it out of my mouth how old I was, my husband said well she's 18. I was so scared I didn't know how old I was. He said, do you have a ring. So, he pulled that ring out of his pocket and gave it to 'em. And he looked it over and turned it over and over and looked at it and pretty soon he looked up and he said well ma'am, I don't think this ring is any good. Oh my land, I just, I almost fainted, here borrowing that ring. I was so scared somethin' would happen to it. He said this ring is no good. Pretty soon he seen I was as green as grass and…didn't even think about a ring not being no good. So, I guess he could see that I was just scared to death. Pretty soon he said well I guess we can use it. So, he put that ring on and we was married. I was just so thrilled about it. I didn't get my first ring until about five years afterwards. *(Correction: The note in the ring box says 1935, three years later.)* It cost $5. But it's a pretty little ring. I still have it…well my granddaughter has it. It's got little orange blossoms around it. Well it's 14 carat gold so I guess it's not too bad. It's just a little band ring but it's pretty.

Chapter Three

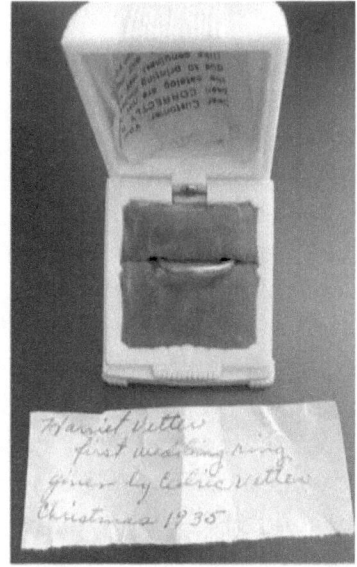

So, we got married and stayed with his aunt that night in town because it was so bad out, it was so cold. The next day we went home. We got home along in the evening to his house. So my mother-in-law she had one room all fixed up for us. She wouldn't hardly let us go in there 'cause I think the brother-in-laws they had went in there and they put big blocks of wood under the mattress. About that big around (holding hands at 12"). That's the reason she didn't want us to go in there and see that bed all humped up. Anyway, that evening why we went to our room and we…there wasn't much chairs or anything, so we just set down on the bed to take our shoes off and that. We just about got half undressed and all of a sudden we heard this bangin' and they was…they had dishpans and they had all kinds of kettles they was bangin' on you know and makin' all kinds of noise right by the window, right where our room was. Back then they had shivarees. They didn't have showers and receptions and all

Chapter Three

this kind of stuff when you get married. They had a shivaree. They'd all gather, all the neighbors and everything and they was a bunch of them. They was all gathered outside by the window. They'd shoot guns up in the air. Oh, they was just making so much noise it would just nearly deafen' ya. We had to go put our shoes on and dress whatever we had on and then they all came in. It was really just a shower. They brought gifts and this one ole guy, he was just a bachelor, lived up past the…in the holler from us. He gave me a white rabbits foot. He had it all done up in nice tissue paper and in a pretty box all wrapped so pretty and everything and when I opened that it made me mad. I thought he was playing some kinda joke on me. I didn't like it at all. I threw the thing away. He said that he gave it to me for good luck. Well I didn't know, and we didn't want to believe in good luck then. Anyway, he said well, that's for good luck. He liked to have a fit when he found out I threw it away. And I don't know whether they ever found it or not, and I didn't want to have anything to do with it 'cause it didn't seem right to me. I got all kinds of dishes, pots and pans and what have ya.

The shivaree lasted until about four or five in the morning. They stayed and stayed until the last minute until they finally left at about five o'clock in the morning or somethin' like that. When we went to get married, the in-laws, their anniversary was on the 28th and they wanted us to wait and get married on their anniversary. We wouldn't do it. We wanted to get married on the 26th. So, we got married the day after Christmas.

Chapter Three

We lived with his folks for I don't know how long, along towards spring. I wanted a home. I wanted a home of my own. I just kept buggin' him. We'll we didn't even have to pay rent. We got this little shack. It was a shack. And it had a dirt floor, one room and so he went and bought some furniture from an old bachelor that was about to die, but anyway it was a homemade table, a bench and a little cook stove about this big, (about 20") it had four, what do you call them? Four places to cook on. A little oven. It was a wood stove. I had a homemade cupboard to put my dishes in and my mother-in-law gave us a bed and we had an army cot and that was our furniture. This dirt floor, I took the shovel and scraped it down or take a knife or anything, I'd scrape it down real smooth and then I'd sweep it. I got that thing as if it were as shiny as it could be. That ole clay dirt it's just real hard and every time you sweep it, it would be shiny. I had it all even and shined up and I made him some curtains out of flour sacks or some kind of material. I had windows about this long and this wide (approximately 12" X 24"). I had two, two little windows. So, I made curtains for that and then the men were farmin' some ground up on the hill from us.

I didn't have a clock and I could cook when I was home, I was a good cook but when I was married it seemed I had forgotten everything. I couldn't think. I went to make biscuits for lunch and I didn't put anything in them but water and flour. They was as hard as a brick and I was afraid that I wouldn't get lunch on time. I just…when they came in at noon, I think they had watches, I didn't know time. I just told time by the sun, but anyway I was afraid I wouldn't have

Chapter Three

lunch on the table. They came in and them biscuits was as hard as bricks and my brother-in-laws they teased me all of the time. They said well you could knock a bull down with 'em. They was just so hard. So, I got through that and my father-in-law, if it hadn't of been for him, I wouldn't have gotten through that. I cried and he said well next time watch what you're doin' and not worry about 'em. About mid spring, we didn't live there very long my brother-in-law came after me to take me back home with him, he came on a horse or team and wagon, and I wasn't quite ready and some way or another I either had a button off or something that I had to pin and I had a little gold safety pin in my mouth open. He was hurrying me up and teasing me and everything and we got in that wagon and he just drove them horses as hard as he could, didn't even have a seat, you had to stand up, and I swallowed that pin. So, when my first son was born, he was such a little ole thing and his head was so little, they always called him pinhead. I don't know, we never did find the pin.

But anyway, we then finally moved back home with them and well that time why, well not right at that time, but there was a time when I had my first baby, and then all the kids home and everything there was ten of the kids and two grandma and grandpa and then me and it just added up and at one time there was sixteen in the family that we had to cook for. And I can remember this big ole bread pan about this big (about 24") it was a square bread pan. It just fit into the wood stove and we'd make them biscuits and make another pan to have enough for everybody. Sixteen, why it takes quite a bit of food.

Chapter Three

Long, oh I don't know how... Jim wasn't sure able to tell yet (with first child). I don't know how long it was after we was married that I got homesick and wanted to go home. So, my husband said well we don't have any way to go, we didn't have a car or anything you know. So, we didn't have any way to go home. I was so homesick, I told him I was gonna start out walkin'. And it was about 50 miles. So, I said well I'm gonna start out walkin'. He said well I don't have any way to take you only you can ride a horse. Well I never ridden a horse before, so I said well, okay, I'll go. His team of horses he had they was great big horses; I don't know how many ton they weighed but they was big. But he couldn't, that's the reason we had to live with his folks, 'cause he couldn't take the team away from his dad 'cause he didn't have any, you know and that's the only way they had to farmin'.

So I said well I'll go, but this particular day that I wanted to go home, I think it was on, I don't know, Sunday, why they were all out there talking you know the guys. Somebody said well, they was gonna go to a ball game. And oh my land, I was just about ready to fight. I said you don't have any way to take me home, but you can go to a ball game. And I went out there and he was standin' on the...where the well was, he had a pump and there was concrete. And I went out there and just tore his vest off. Boy I was pretty riled up. I was really mad 'cause he wouldn't take me home. I can't even remember if he went on...I think he did, he went on to the ball game. He just left me. He should of just stayed home. But anyway, that next day or so why he went out and we didn't even have a saddle on the horse either. It was just a bareback it had a blanket on it. It didn't have a saddle on it

Chapter Three

or anything. And I rode that 50 miles and never got off. The whole time. And he'd get off and walk you know. But I sat there all the time. It was hard enough to get up there on that horse without gettin' climbin' up and down all the time. I was pregnant so we got to my mother's home and so I had to stay about three weeks before I was able to come home. They had to put me to bed, they had to carry me in the house, I couldn't move. So, I stayed about three weeks before I was able to come home. Then he went back home with the horse and next time why he borrowed a car to come after me. It was something else.

Then I think it was after that, my two sister-in-laws and my brother-in-laws, they was, I tell you they treated me mean. One Sunday they was gonna go horseback riding. Well I didn't want no part of horseback riding but they was generous enough to want me to go. They didn't want to leave me behind. They wanted me to go and I didn't want to, but my sister-in-law says, well, I'll ride with you. She'll take care of me. Yeah, she took care of me all right. She went in the barn and she got this old blind horse… ole blind Bill. Saddled 'em for me to ride. She said well I'll get on with you, I'll ride with ya. She got to that horse, to runnin' real fast. Although the horse was blind, you know, he could run. Scared me to death, I nearly fell off. Oh, I was so mad at her I nearly choked her. Me pregnant and her runnin' that horse like that, oh I was so mad at her. But they'd do all kinds of tricks like that on me. I don't know why but then my father-in-law said, well if they didn't love you, they wouldn't tease you like that. And I said well they must love me an awful lot because they was always doing something to

Chapter Three

torment me, and to tease me and to play jokes on me. They had all kinds of problems or they did all kinds of things to me.

So all that time, I think from the time I got pregnant until my first son was born, I had malaria fever, and I didn't eat as much as you could put on a little plate the whole time. I was just well, nothing but skin and bones in the first place and then when he was born, he only weighed five and a half pounds. The funny thing about it, well it seemed funny at the time…I get to thinkin' about it and it was pretty awful…my first one was a boy and his daddy wouldn't even come in the room and look at 'em. It was three days 'for he came in to see 'em. I didn't know why; I just never did find out why he didn't come in to see the baby, but he wouldn't. At the same time my sister-in-law and that friend that took us to get married, why they was married then and she lost her first baby. She came home and she was in the living room on a day bed and I was in the bedroom in my room. She wanted to see the baby and wanted to come see me. She just wrapped the sheet all around her and came in there and liked to scared me to death. I thought it was a ghost or somethin'. She came in wrapped up in that sheet and liked to of scared me to death.

Then I think Glen was about two years old, we went to this place where we was gonna harvest the corn. I went along to do the cookin'. Well I wouldn't leave the kids with my mother-in-law, I had to take them along. Well he would have been two years old the next day. We got up about oh, four o'clock in the morning. He always got up when we did. I

Chapter Three

just had a flannel gown on him, well when he got up, his daddy put some little coveralls over that flannel gown. We had a great big long bench and I had breakfast ready. I had just pored coffee that you cook on an old wood stove you know, and it was hot as it could be. That bench was one leg shorter than the other. Well when he climbed up on that bench why it tipped over you know and just spilled half of that cup of coffee. It just burned em all over, 'specially all along his side he just got real big scars on 'em now. His face was all burned. Well nobody ate breakfast, we just started out and took him to the doctor. We had to cross the river, cause the river was high and we had to go in a boat. The ferry didn't run so we went over to town in that boat. The ole doctor, he put carbolic salve all over 'em and that's the worse thing you can do for a burn. And he had convulsions. I don't know how many he had but he just kept havin' 'em one right after another. We took him to another doctor, and he put some different stuff on him. We just about lost him. Two years old he had to learn to walk all over again. He was really bad. Then my second baby was only three months old. There was only 21 months different in their ages. She was three months old. But anyway, we had a hard time with him.

It was really a hard life with sixteen of us in the family and I had to cook and worsh on the board; it was really just hard times. Not only the work, but we didn't have much food, it was still in the depression like you know and we didn't have any food and my sister-in-law and I, we went out under a pear tree and it was in November and it had just begin to kinda frost good, and these pears was all under these leaves. So we went out there and dug these pears out, and if you

Chapter Three

want something good, ya take these pears and fry them in butter and I tell you that is so delicious. But that's what we had for breakfast. We had butter, but we didn't have any meat or anything like that, so we fried pears and they were really good.

Then we moved again. I think we moved about every time I turned around. We was movin' 'cause I was wantin' a home of my own. We moved again and my third son (or my third child) was born. Fifteen months after. There was fifteen months difference between my daughter and this one. And the ole doctor that we had, we called him about oh, along in the morning...early morning. He came and said well just let nature take its course, so he went up on the hill squirrel huntin' and he didn't come down. I was so aggravated that he didn't stay with me. It seemed like it was hours that he stayed up there. Anyway, he finally came down and he weighed fifteen pounds. The first one was five and a half pounds, the next one was what, seven and something and this one weighed.... No I'm wrong, it was twelve and a half pounds. That's a little better. Twelve and a half pounds he weighed.

Well before he was born though, why we lived in this house and they had seed wheat all on this front porch. We couldn't get out the front door, we had to go around through the kitchen and we had to go around to get to the front porch. I missed Glenn. He was just a little bittie ole thing. I went to look for him and hollerin' for him and I couldn't find him no place, so I went out... this was just before my third one was born and I went out there, and there his feet, just about

Chapter Three

this much of his feet was hangin' out, one of them big hundred pound wheat, sacks of wheat had fell on him he'd climbed up the steps and went up there where that wheat was and that sacks of wheat rolled over on 'em. That's all that was stickin' out was just his feet. So, I ran up them steps and I took that hundred pound of wheat and I lifted it off of 'em and how I did it I don't know 'cause wheat is really heavy. So, I brought 'em in the house. But that was just a startin' I guess in life. Hard times with the kids it seemed like every time you turn around there was somethin' happenin' to every one of them.

Then one day it came a real bad storm. Course we had a whole lot of lights, lamps and uh, but anyway this storm come up and it was just awful. And I had to go to the cellar to get potatoes for supper. And It was two doors that opened up on the outside of the porch. Why there was these two doors that opened up that you went down into the cellar. It wasn't a basement; it was a cellar. I forgot that your supposed to hook that door to keep it from goin' down you know shuttin'. I forgot to do that, the wind was blowin' and everything and I was hurryin' down there to get potato's for supper so when I was down there, the wind blew that door shut and it was stuck so tight that I couldn't even open it. They was a window oh about this big and this high (2x2) and I was about to give birth to another baby and that's the only way I had getting out. I climbed up and ya had to climb up a bank like it was just dirt shelf like there to get to the window. I couldn't hardly get up there. Couldn't hardly climb up there. But anyway, I got out that window and came around, I was so afraid that the wind would blow the lamp out and

Chapter Three

these two little other kids was nothing but babies and I was afraid they'd get scared and go to crying and everything in the dark. So I hurried out of that window and I got back in there. I still don't know whether I brought my potatoes up or not, evidently not. That was a real challenge.

Then one day my husband went to work and we had to get up real early in the morning. I fixed his lunch and after he was gone...I never...I didn't worsh dishes. I didn't do anything. I didn't take care of the kids. I didn't do anything. I just started crying. I cried and I cried, and I cried and I tried to pray and I told the Lord I'm lost. I just felt so lost. It was just terrible. I cried and prayed all day long and didn't know what to do. When he came home that night, I think it was about five o'clock in the evening when he got home, I met 'em at the door. Just blubberin', just a bawlin' like crazy. He wanted to know what was going on and I said, well I'm lost, I'm lost. Well, he said no problem there, we can take care of that. So, he told me...I had, then I had my bed in the livin' room. He said just come on over here and set on the bed and he got him a chair and pulled up to the bed. And he read John 3:16 to me, talked to me, and explained you know, everything. And just all of a sudden, I just laid back on the bed and I went to sleep. I don't know how long I slept but it seemed like quite a long time, but I had such peace about me that I just really didn't care whether the world rolled around on me or what, but I was just so peaceful. I suppose that I was just saved ya know, that Lord saved me. All this time I was beggin' em to save me. I didn't know what to do, I didn't know what I was supposed to do or what He was

Chapter Three

supposed to do or what. After he read this John 3:16, I was all right.

But I always, from then on every time I'd go to church, I'd want to go to the alter. Seemed like that they was just something told me that I had to go to the alter. And every time I'd go nothing happened. I sure went through a miserable time and I didn't understand what to do to be saved and I didn't understand the Bible or anything. But anyway, I had peace about me. I was all right.

Then we bought a farm; a 280-acre farm. We only gave $2800.00 for a 280-acre farm, and oh, I was so thrilled that I had a home. We had four rooms and boy I was just really right up town you know. I had this place, and oh, I made curtains, and I still have my curtains that I made out of feed sacks and I trimmed them in green checks. I had a sack that was green checks, so I trimmed 'em in that. I still have 'em. I should of brought them for a show and tell. But anyway, I was really happy on that farm. Well then it wasn't too long my youngest son was two years old when our fourth baby was born, and it was stillborn. So, I had quite a time with that, but anyway we moved again off the farm to another place where they was farmin' about a thousand acres or somethin' like that. We moved. It was a ranch. So, we moved again.

Then my daughter that's here, Sharon, was born about five years later. She was born there, well when she was born, she was about 8 days old, I took real bad kidney infection. They didn't think I was gonna make it, but I did. They took a

Chapter Three

hundred pounds of ice and just packed me in hundred pounds of ice. I was too sick to move me to the hospital. So, I think I was sick for about three weeks, somthin' like that and I finally came out of it. But anyway, Sharon, she wouldn't take a bottle or anything and she wouldn't eat. Her daddy would take her thumb and put it in her mouth. Wasn't any nourishment in that, but then anyway he just got her started suckin' her thumb. She sucked her thumb for I don't know how long, she won't want to hear any of that. She won't want to listen to this. I got over that. Then three and a half years later, I had this other still born baby. Before I was thirty, I had six children. This last one was born on 23rd of April and I would have been thirty on the thirtieth of April. By the time I was 30 we had six children and I lost two of them.

We, I guess was married about ten years and we was still on this ranch. I don't even like to think about this part of it, but I was mean as the Devil himself. And you know how mean he is. I was mad at the whole world. I plotted and I planned. I did everything under the sun to kill my whole family. I was an attempted murderer, I guess that's what you'd call me. And I'm not proud of it at all. I don't like to think about how awful mean I was. But I was mad at everybody and just mean to the kids and I'd knock them around and I'd whip 'em and I was so mean. I was so mad at my husband I wouldn't even talk to 'em. So, one day I thought well I'll go to the levy. The water was real high and they had a levy up there. I thought I'd go down to the levy and I'd just drown myself. I got down there, and I couldn't even…I was chicken. I couldn't do that to myself, but yet I could plot

Chapter Three

and plan on killin' the rest of 'em. The kids were all real little. I think Glen was 'bout, oh he couldn't have been over eight or somthin' like that. The rest of them was all littler. They had corn on each side of the road that went to the levy. It was real tall corn and you couldn't see over it you know if you stood on the ground. Them kids got up on top of the car so they could see me, and they just cried. Said oh mommy don't leave us. Don't leave us. And they would just cry and tell me oh, come back, please don't leave us. So, I didn't. I didn't even want to go back. I was goin' down there to kill myself or drown myself or whatever I could do. So, I got down there, and I was just too chicken to do it. I didn't want to do that, so I came back home, and I was still real mad at 'em. Wouldn't talk to nobody. I was just real hateful. Temper…I had a temper like you'd never believe.

We'll stop there. That's the end of this chapter. But the next chapter is a new complete new life. Praise the Lord. Complete new life. So, I'll leave you there so you can think about the new life. The new wonderful, wonderful life. That God just changed me completely and I just praise the Lord from every day I thank 'em and praise 'em and I said he gave me a new life. You know the Bible just says that if any man be in Christ Jesus, he is a new creature, old things pass away, and all things become new. And that's exactly what happened to me. It was completely new. All this old temper, all this ole wantin' to murder everybody…kill everybody, all went away was completely a new life. The next time it gets really exciting. So, I thank you.

Chapter Four

October 22, 1997

Just to backtrack just a little bit here before we go into this new life that I told you about. When my last baby was born, I wasn't gettin' along too good. The doctor told me I had to have a hysterectomy. I went and had that done. And when I came home, I just was real sick. I think I was in the hospital for about three weeks. I was real sick. I couldn't even walk from one room to the other without hurtin' so bad. But the doctors had told my husband that I had cancer, but he didn't tell me. He wouldn't tell me for a long, long time after that. I guess I was pretty sick person because I wasn't able to do anything hardly. My neighbors had come in. Four H girls had come in and done all my canning. They canned tomatoes and everything in the garden and my neighbor she came and helped with the cookin' and everything while I was in the hospital. Maybe that was one reason that I was so mean and was so mad at everybody and I was as mean as the ole Devil himself. But the water was high. The river was high, and we couldn't get across the river to go to the church we always went to. And my husband, he'd go to church anyplace, didn't make any difference what church it was, he'd go to church. So, he started to go to Assembly of God. We were always Baptist, didn't make any difference to him. He never leaned to the denomination anyway.

Chapter Four

Harriet and Cedric (Shad) Vetter

He went to this Assembly of God and got acquainted with the pastor and the pastor was a woman and her husband. So, one night they came to see us and the store where they lived, would have a lot of lettuce and carrots and things like that leftover that they couldn't sell, and they had rabbits. So, the store would give it to them for the rabbits. Some of it would

Chapter Four

be really good. They would sort it out and clean it up and ever' thing and they'd bring us carrots and lettuce and I don't know what all. They came to see us that day and they was talking to us about going to a healin' meeting. Of course, I was mad at everybody and I said I don't want to go. I had all kinds of excuses you know that I didn't want to go. Well my husband was blind in one eye. They said well, I think maybe if you'd go, why he'd be healed in his blind eye. He said he wouldn't go without me. I was too stubborn to even say I was gonna go. I wouldn't go and all this kinda stuff. So finally, they talked me into goin'. I didn't think about goin'. I didn't know anything about healing. I didn't think about needin' healin' myself. They finally talked me into goin'.

This was in Louisiana, MO. We drove, oh my I don't know how many hours it took us to get there. We started out 'long in the afternoon. Got to the meeting that night. Well, goin' up there why this pastor she said, well you know I think you'd be good to work with the young people. I said no, I'm not fit to work with anything. I don't want to work with anybody. I'm not fit for anything. She kept talking to me you know and pretty soon I said all I want, all I want at all is to just have more of the Lord. Right then, that was just a sort of a, well I can't explain what it was, but I knew that the Lord was dealing with me in some way. And I begin to think about that I really did need more of the Lord. I felt like I was saved even as mean as I was. I did feel like I was saved, but then I just didn't, I knew they was something wrong, I needed somethin'. So that's what I said, I said well, I just need more of the Lord. Well, I know that she was a sittin' there praying just as hard as she could, prayin' for me.

Chapter Four

We got to the meeting. Oh, there was a big crowd. The preacher, brother Brown (he's gone a long time). Anyway, he was the pastor, preacher evangelist. He preached for a little while and pretty soon he said well, we don't have time to pray for everybody individually. We want everybody to just come through the prayer line. About that time this lady was sittin' down close to the front and she'd started screamin' and just, it was just terrible. Making a lot of noise and screamin' real loud and everything and he looked down and said well we have a lady here that is full of demons. Well I never heard anything about demons. I didn't know what a demon was from a rat. So, he said that he was gonna cast them demons out of her. And he said now if there is anybody here that don't believe in this, why I want you to get up and go outside. I want you to just leave, he says now, if you don't believe in it…in that, why he said if you want to stay, you better start prayin' because them demons might come into you. Well I started to prayin'. I tell you I prayed, I never prayed so hard in my life quite yet. I just started to prayin' real hard. I didn't want them demons to come into me. All of a sudden, the shutters on the windows begin to rattle and it was just terrible. It was just like an earthquake. He told us he said well that's the demons going out of the windows. Boy I was scared to pieces. I was just really scared. I just kept on prayin'. She laid in the floor for I guess the rest of the meeting. It was pretty late. Well it was three o'clock back when we got home.

Anyway, when it was gettin' late like ten o'clock he said well, he wanted everybody to go through the prayer line. Not come up for him to pray for us individually, but just go

Chapter Four

through the prayer line. Well, we went and my husband and I both went through the prayer line. We didn't even touch the preacher or anything, didn't shake his hand or anything. We just went through the prayer line and it was a pretty long line. So, we went home. It was real late when we got home.

They had a revival at this church that he'd been goin' to. So, they asked us to come to the revival and I think that was on a Monday night when we went up there and maybe Tuesday night we went to the revival at her church. So we came home and nothing happened. I didn't feel any different than I did before. Well I was a little bit better than I was. I wasn't quite as mad at everybody and I wasn't still plottin' on killin' or anything. So, I think I was better. I kept thinkin' about this, what I said that I just wanted *more of the Lord*. I knew then that something was goin' on with me and the Lord. I knew he was trying to tell me something. We went all through the next day. Well the next evening, that next night, we was gonna go to the revival. I didn't have any clothes fit hardly to wear anyplace. Somebody had given me high-heel shoes. I know they was that high *(holding fingers at 3 inches)* so, I put them on, and I dressed the best I could. I remember though I had a dress. Just a plain dress that I had caught it under a barbed wire fence or somethin' tore a hole in it. Well, I patched it back there *(shoulder)*. You couldn't tell too much about I had a patch on it. Anyway, I put that dress on.

So, there was a friend of ours that wanted to take the kids to a movie. So, Sharon my youngest daughter was about four years old…well she wasn't quite four years old yet and then three others so they wanted to take 'em to the show. I didn't

Chapter Four

think anything about it 'till we got to the place to this town where we supposed to leave them off to go to the show and we got in the car to go with the other preacher to go on to this other town. I guess it was about 20 miles all together. And when them kids got out of the car to go to the show, something just came over me and I said well I don't like this. Part of the family going one way and part the other. It just didn't strike me good. Them kids was goin' to the show and we was going to the revival. I hated to leave 'em 'cause they was all pretty, well I think the oldest was eight or nine, maybe older. I guess the Lord just started to workin' in me.

We got to the revival and they sang several songs and the preacher got up to preach and she said well I'm gonna preach on the baptism of the Holy Spirit. She hadn't gotten I don't know, five minutes into her sermon, when we came in, we had to sit right on the second seat from the front. 'Course I didn't like that. I liked one back there behind somebody where nobody could see me. That was the only seat open, so we had to sit in the second seat from the front. About five minutes after that I jumped up just as bold as you could get and I said, well sister friend, I think I've got what you're talkin' about. She says well praise the Lord sister, and says why don't you come to the altar and thank the Lord for it. Well I didn't know what I had, but I knew there was something goin' stern in my heart. I went to the altar and I knelt down, and it was a little ole church that they had a light on a cord hanging down. And it was only a, I don't think it was over 60 or 70 watt. But anyway, it wasn't very bright. I got down there, and I started a prayin' and I thanked the

Chapter Four

Lord for my family and I thanked 'em that I was saved and that's about all I knew to thank 'em for.

All of a sudden, they was a, it was just like they turned on more lights. It was just such a bright light that came down and I just said, oh my! It was so bright that it almost hurt your eyes. And I kinda opened one eye and peaked up there to see if they had turned on another light and they didn't. There was that same still little ole light bulb hangin' down there. Oh my, the Lord just flooded my life with just brightness. Brighter than anything I've ever seen in my life. And I started speakin' in tongues. Well, I couldn't...I tried to think well what's happinin' to me. I was too...well I don't know how to explain it. I was just in a...the Lord was just blessin' me so that I couldn't figure out what was goin' on. I started speakin' in tongues. Well I had heard that they said, "Oh, these Pentecostal people, you go down there" and said, "they'll lay their hands on you and they'll push you over and they'll say a word you know just real fast so you...you know if you say anything real fast to anybody, why you get so you do it too." And that's what they told me, that's what tongues was. I knew better that this is something more than that, so I started speakin' in tongues. I just began to...the power of God was just flowing all over me. Just flowing. It was like a river. Just runnin'. The longer I went the better it got. I can't even begin to tell you how I felt. Finally, by that time it was two hours that had passed by and I was still up at the altar. Finally, I got up from the altar and I went back to my seat and I just kept jumping up and testifying. They couldn't keep me down. They couldn't even tie me down. She never did get to preach and everybody else was all stirred up. They was

Chapter Four

testifying, saying they knew something happened to me and they knew what it was. Every time anybody would say anything, well here I'd pop up and almost interrupt them and go to tell them…I'd go to tell them, well I've been a Baptist all my life and I've never had anything like this happen to me. I was just really full.

Then we went back that same night. Church lasted oh, I don't know eleven or twelve o'clock, I guess. People was just testifyin' and talking and everything. Of course, they couldn't keep me down. I was doin most of it. That same night when we got ready to go home, why we came with this other pastor. About halfway home, I think we had to walk about three miles from where the car was, all the wires burned off of it. Every wire. We didn't have lights it wouldn't go; it wouldn't start. Nothing. So, he said well, I don't know if there is anything else that we can do, but just have to walk home. I had them big ole high-heels and I said hang on folks, I believe I can fly. So, I told them I said you just hang on I believe I can fly. I tell you…It's just hard to explain what happened to me. Anyway, we started home 'bout three miles to our car. I was just so, the spirit was just upon me it was so great that I felt like I could do anything. I did, I felt like I could fly. We was walkin' along you know and they was complainin' about their feet hurtin' them you know, walkin' that far and everything and here I had them big ole high-heel shoes on and I was just a walkin' along just never even paying attention to 'em. Why any other time I couldn't hardly walk in them 'cause I wasn't used to wearin' them high heels. But anyway, as we walked, I saw the face of Jesus just right up from me you know on the right side, just his face. Then I

Chapter Four

felt him take a hold of my hand and lead me. He just was smiling and just walking right along with me, just going with me. Then all of a sudden, I saw what seemed like just the whole universe, I saw my name written in the sky. My name was written down in the lamb's book of life. Well I wasn't there; I was about 10-feet-high or more than that. I remember though that it was about three weeks, when I came down to earth. I actually bounced. I was so full of the spirit; wasn't here on earth at all. I was up here enjoying all this good stuff that happened to me. I was just so happy. I'd never been so happy in my life. So there Jesus was holdin' to my hand just leading me along. Finally, we got to the town where we left our car and we picked the kids up. Of course, the show had been out for a long, long time and they was sittin' on the porch and all of them was asleep sittin' on that porch. This was in August. I remember the day and the hour that this happened to me. It was August the 19th in 1946 about eight o'clock at night and I tell you, it was just so wonderful that I just couldn't hardly contain it all.

So then on Wednesday night, they asked me to lead prayer meeting. Why I had never done anything like that. I was so bashful and so timid that I couldn't even pray or anything. I was so timid that anybody look at me or stick their finger in my face, why I'd cry. I just couldn't believe that they'd ask me to lead the prayer meeting. Well I didn't care. It didn't matter to me. I just said OK. I went home and I just started. What will I talk about, what will I say? Although I was willing, the Lord told me he said, *well, talk about love*. I got my Bible and I went…and started through it. I said well I'll talk about the love of God. That was the main thing. Then the

Chapter Four

love that a husband and wife has between them, and then the love of your children, and the love that we should have for one another as Christians, our brothers and sisters, the love for one another. I put that sermon together and I tell you, they thought that some great evangelist had come in. They just went on and on and on. Well it wasn't me. I didn't do it. The Lord just spoke through me you know. Just as fast as I could talk, I'd just talk, and I'd give 'em all these scriptures what this said about that. What another scripture said about lovin' like your husband or your children. I just talked about love the whole thing through. I think they had to stop me. I just never did get thru. Anyway, that was my first time that I had done anything. Although we'd been going to this church, I wouldn't do nothin'. I was like a knot on a log. I wouldn't do anything.

But anyway, I wanted to mention about when we got home that first night when I got the baptism of the Holy Spirit. We went to bed and it was, I'd say about three o'clock in the morning when we got home. We was just layin' there talking about what had happened. All of a sudden, they was these little, I guess they was demons. I don't know what they was, but they was little devils. Anyway sittin' all around the foot of the bed and all around me. They was just everyplace. Just little bitty ole things. We'd talk about different things you know what we knew about...well I never knew that they was such a thing about the baptism of the Holy Spirit. My husband, although he was a Baptist all his life, he really believed it, he'd believe the Bible. He didn't go to anybody else or any church or anything. He took his Bible and he believed what the Bible said. I started to feel this side of my

Chapter Four

stomach (left). It felt as light as a feather. It was so light you didn't even know I had anything there. And this side was just as heavy as a ton of brick (right). It was just so heavy. And I said well Lord I saw that they was something happening. I said Lord, if I've doubted you in any way that you could heal me, well I want you to forgive me, 'cause I know you can heal me. Well before, you know, I didn't know anything about healing. But the Bible says in Isaiah 53:5 it says, *But He was wounded for our transgressions, He was bruised for our iniquities; the chastisement for our peace was upon Him, and by His stripes we are healed.* Well I began to soak in, and I began to believe that, and I knew that that's what the Bible said. That by the stripes of Jesus that he took on his back we are healed. I told him, Lord, I know that you can heal me. I don't want to doubt you in any way. So, we went to sleep. The next morning when we got up, why this side that had been heavy, it was just as light as a feather. I was just light all over. Like light as a feather I guess. That's the only way I know how to say how light I was.

I was just, oh, I'd get up in the morning you know and before, I had nine men to cook for and nine coon hounds. It just took all day long cookin' and worshin' dishes that's all you got done, besides me and four kids. I got up that morning. I got everything done in no time. I got my Bible and I went out on that porch and I started reading it and I couldn't get enough of it. I just read, and I read, and I read it seemed like it just all was so good. I couldn't stop you know. Then I'd come in and I tried to do something else. I had to cook for them big ole dogs, them big ole coon dogs. I had a great big pot to put on the back of the wood stove. I'd put

Chapter Four

table scraps in it. Then we'd take crackling's and we'd take corn meal and everything to make up this food for 'em. Always before I'd even put that food out there for 'em when it was hot. I didn't care whether they burned their mouth or anything. But you know I began to love them ole dogs. I just loved them to pieces. My husband says, well I know something happened to you now that you love my dogs; and before I hated them. I hated them dogs. They barked all the time. Of course, they had them pinned up you know. They were real good coon hounds, some of them was worth $500. I hated them ole dogs and I'd put their food out hot and I wouldn't care if they got burned on it or what. After the Holy Spirit, why it seemed like I just loved them ole dogs. I'd go out there and I'd pet 'em you know and talk to 'em. There was a drastic change. Anyway, he was so proud to think that I loved his dogs.

When everybody was in the house with me, I'd be alright. But just the minute that everybody would leave, go outside and nobody would be around, I'd feel something tapping me on the shoulder and I'd look around and nobody would be there. I'd go on doin' something else and pretty soon tapping on the shoulder. Finally, I'd detected that it was just the devil trying to torment me. I could feel 'em so strong. I'd rebuke him you know, and I didn't even know how to do anything like that before. I'd say devil you get out of here you get out of my site. You're not gonna bother me. I just want you to go, and I'd think about Jesus when he was, when the devil would torment 'em and he'd say well, get behind me satan. Well, that's what I'd say is get behind me satan, you get out of here. You leave this place, I'm not gonna put up with it. I

Chapter Four

was just so brave, why I was willing to talk to anybody that was trying to harm me. Soon as everybody come in, why I'd be alright I didn't feel that.

Anyway, as I say three weeks I was up in the air, cloud twelve, not cloud nine, cloud twelve. When I came down to earth, I just actually bounced. My mother-in-law and some of my sister-in-laws, they disowned me. They wouldn't talk to me and they didn't want to have anything to do with me. They said awe, she's crazy. She must have gone crazy. Well I don't know whether I'm crazy or not, but if that's what crazy is, why I want to be this way all my life. So, I didn't mind it at all.

The Church that we always went to, they was gonna have a, the doors was closed, but anyway somebody had got together, it was the 50th anniversary of the church and they was gonna open that up. The Lord gave me a vision and it was so wonderful how God can just tell you and give you a vision of what he wants you to do. He was gonna start my life out right. Anyway, in this vision I could see he showed me these little round back chairs that was in the church. I don't know how many they was, but they was all in a circle. So, he told me he said he wanted me to start teaching there and teaching the beginners. I could just see them just all in a circle like that. He told me he said I want you to start with the beginners and I want you to go from there on up to the next class and on up and teach all the classes. Well I did that in a year or so. I taught the little ones. We had a ball. We'd go out on nature walks and we'd be just in this one room country church. I'd think maybe we would disturb the other

Chapter Four

classes, so I'd take 'em outside and we'd have nature walks and I'd tell them how God made everything, the butterflies and spiders and everything. Oh, I just enjoyed it so much. It wasn't too long ago, I was back in Illinois and we had a reunion. They was five of the little ones. Well they was big then but what I mean was the ones that I taught. They said oh, we just remember them classes that you taught us and the nature walks and all that kind of stuff. It just thrilled my heart to think that I did do good. The Church named Pleasant Dale. It was a little white church and the Lord was so good to us. We just enjoyed that so much.

Anyway, the day of this 50th anniversary, my husband got up and asked how many people would be willing to come back to the church, and open up the doors, and have church, and have Sunday school and we'd start that back up again. Well, they was nine people that would come back and we'd start it back up again. I remember having about twenty-five little ones in my class. The beginners class. That was quite a big amount to have for a country church.

So, then we moved back to the farm. I was telling you earlier we bought the farm and then we moved over into this other Mississippi bottoms where we could farm about, well I think at one time it was about 1000 acres. We moved back to the farm in 1949 and my husband was ordained to be a pastor. Although he had preached all his life, or ever since he was big enough to preach and he went to evangelistic school in Chicago, he just never had been ordained. In the Baptist church you had to be ordained in the church and everything

Chapter Four

just right before you could get up and preach. I didn't get my ordination, but then I sure got up and preached.

The first time we went to our first church, my husband didn't even have a suit. He just had an old grey pair of work pants and an ole suit coat that he had way back. He didn't mind just as long as he was clean, that's all he cared. We opened up three doors of three churches and one schoolhouse. The first day we went, we had to sell a couple dozen eggs to get gas enough to go. So, we sold our eggs and we went to this place to preach that Sunday morning. Then next Sunday, we'd go and open up another door. We had this schoolhouse and they was a Methodist preacher came to us one time and he wanted us to have church in this schoolhouse. He wanted me to teach class. I told em, I says well, the only thing wrong was that I just couldn't see. I couldn't see to study; my eyes had gotten so bad. I told him I just can't see to study. We had a what they called a one-day revival once a month. It had a revival and they would go from one church to another. It didn't make any difference whether they was Methodist, Baptist, Presbyterian, Catholic, Lutheran, any church they would welcome. We'd go there once a month and we'd have a one-day revival. They'd call on me at just the last minute to read the scripture, to pray, or do something when the meeting first started.

So when the meeting was almost over, they usually let out about four o'clock. He said I want everybody to just open up your purses and I want you to give all you can give. He said I won't tell you what it is for, but he said it was for a good cause. So, they passed their hats around. They didn't even

Chapter Four

have collection plates or anything. So they passed their hats around. So, they took it back up to 'em. And he told them he said well, he wanted me to teach a class and I couldn't see, and I needed some glasses. So, he just brought the hat back, put it together and brought the hat back and just poured it in my lap. Well they was a lot more than what I needed for glasses. I couldn't even say a word. I couldn't do anything. I just set there and bawled. I just couldn't say anything. I was just so…I just didn't say nothing. He told them, he said well this is for me to get glasses with. I don't think I ever thanked the people, I just couldn't. I couldn't say anything. Anyway, that's the way it was, every month we'd have this revival and they'd call on me to do something. They had all these other preachers that preached for years and they'd call on me to open up the service.

Well my husband was blind in one eye, but he had this real bad heart problem. His one valve of his heart was grown shut and the other side leaked. He had rheumatic fever when he was a kid. It just didn't you know, he had a hard time. Sometimes he'd get up on Sunday morning and he couldn't speak, but a whisper. Sometimes he couldn't even whisper. So, he always called me momma. He'd say momma you're gonna have to take the service this morning. Well I didn't no more think anything about it or nothin'. I'd just grab my Bible and sometimes I'd take some of his notes whatever he had and sometimes I wouldn't. Most of the time I wouldn't. But I'd just get it all together and go to this church and I'd preach. They all thought I had been at it for years. But anyway, I didn't think anything about it. I'd just grab my Bible and away we'd go.

Chapter Four

Right at that time, it was still the depression or felt the effects of it and we had gas rationing. We had cards to get so much gas. That's the way we got our gas to go to the meetings. And of course all the boys went to....well earlier though when we lived in the bottoms, why all the boys and our hired hands went to war. I had four brothers that went to war and I had three brother-in-laws and of course all of our hired hands, they all went. We just had to do the best we could. You know, do all the work ourselves. I had to get out and I had to do a lot on the farm. I baled hay and I drove tractors and I chopped wood and I done everything. But anyway, we made it. I remember we picked apples for about the time we'd go to these churches. I picked apples all week long and then I bought me a new dress that I could wear to go to these churches. It was a pretty rough life, but I had the Lord and that's all I cared and all I wanted, I had the Lord. He was so good to me.

My husband died when he was 42 years old, We'd been married like in three months being 19 years, or 20 years. He passed away and I know he went to be with the Lord. The church moved me out to town. I was up on that big ole farm and I couldn't run the farm and the kids wasn't big enough to do it. They moved me to town. I scrubbed floors and I worshed on the board and I done irons and done a little bit of everything to send the kids to school. But I finally got them all, you know, to send 'em to school. My youngest son, he left home when he was fifteen and went to this Nazarene college in Kankakee, Illinois and he lived in the attic of somebody's house. You couldn't hardly stand up, of course he was tall, he couldn't hardly stand up he'd hit the ceiling.

Chapter Four

He'd eat cheese and crackers. He'd work wherever he could. Work in a hotel and today he has his bachelor degree, his master's degree and all of these degrees you can get. So, he knows how he got his education. He'd send his clothes home so he could worsh and iron, but I didn't have hardly the money to send 'em back to him. Anyway, they all got a good education. I cleaned house and did a little bit of everything to send the kids to school.

It wasn't a year or so and I got married again. I just thought I needed somebody to help me raise kids, I wasn't thinking about anything else. I didn't even pray about this second marriage. I got in bad trouble. That marriage lasted almost seven years. He took his own life. I had gotten him a rifle for his birthday, and he killed himself with that rifle. That marriage I just like to kind of put it way over here down the hill where I don't want to think about it anymore. God was so good to me and worked things out to where I just try to not talk about it. I just don't want to talk about it. It is just two painful. It's too hard. They was a lot of things involved that I won't even mention it was just terrible. But God was so gracious and so good to me that he gave me a mind that most anybody would have went crazy then. But I had the Lord, so I had to just go on. I had Sharon that was, oh about fifteen or something like that. I just had to make the best of it. I was working at the State Hospital and I was just doing the best I could, but it was just hard.

Then it wasn't too long after that I met this other guy *(Kenneth Hankla)*. But believe me, I prayed about that. I really prayed and I asked the Lord, is this what you want? I didn't want to

Chapter Four

do it oh, just for myself. Just wanted to know whether it was right with the Lord. He was a jewel. He was really a good man. So, I lived with him. We was married almost six years and he died of cancer. I took care of him all by myself. I didn't have any help and the last four months of his life, he was in the hospital and he wanted to come home and he wanted to die at home and be with me. So, I took him home and the doctor said woman, you're crazy, he said you cannot take care of that man. I said, well that's what he wants. Every time I went to the hospital he'd cry and want to come home. So, I just went and told the doctors, you know, I'm gonna take him home and I'm gonna take care of 'em. They said you must be crazy, you can't take care of him. Do you realize it's a 24-hour job? I said yeah, I know, I'll take care of him if I had to crawl to do it. I didn't know what I was sayin' cause I practically ended up crawling to take care of 'em. I didn't have any help. So, he died December, well we buried him on Christmas Eve. I guess it was the 21st when he died. He was a good Christian man. What little life they was, I had a good life with him. And I know that he's with the Lord now. That was very hard on me. I had lost so much weight that I had a real nice coat and when I went to put it on for his funeral, it just hung on me like a big ole sack. It was so big for me. I couldn't leave him. I never went to get my hair fixed. I just looked like an old hag for sure. I got through it. So here I am.

But anyway, the Lord was so good to me. I think about where the Lord brought me from and how he brought me into this new life. It was a complete new life that I lived and I still live and it gets better every day. The psalm says Jesus

Chapter Four

is sweeter every day. My Christian life or my life that I try to live the best way that I know how before people that they might benefit from my life. I don't think about what I say and what I do. I just want people to look at my everyday life and see Jesus in me. Not see me, but I want them to see Jesus in my life. I do the best that I know how. With anything that I do I always bend over backwards to do the best that I can. I want to give God the best that I have. I hope my life is pleasing to him. I want to hear him say one day that *I was a good servant and well done.* That's all that I want to hear. I want to hear Him say that I lived my life for Him.

The next chapter is gonna be mostly of a little bit before I moved here. I've been here fourteen years as of the 28th of this month. It's gonna be full. I don't know whether I can make it through just one session or whether I can have two. But that's what it's gonna be. Mostly of since I've lived here. It's a full life.

Chapter Four

Chapter Four

Harriet Hankla and Mike Wallace - Fathers Day 1988
Denton, Texas

Chapter Five

November 5, 1997

Last time kind of seemed like I was jumping around a little bit from one thing to another. I don't have it in order the way that I did the other. I just want to go over a little bit more of the clothing room. I was telling you that I had the clothing room and all the things that happened there. There is a little bit more that I want to tell about.

In the clothing room we had big bags of beans and dry milk. I had zip lock bags and put milk in the bags, and I would give out to the families. If they was a big family, maybe I'd give them two bags. I did the beans and the dry milk and everything and when big families would come in why we had bread and we had frozen things like chickens, different things in the freezer. That was a big blessing to take care of everybody that came for not only clothes, but food and spiritual food as well. We would pray with the people and see whether they were Christians or what need they had in their life. That was a blessing too. We seen many people that was saved, healed and what have ya'. So, they would be a lot of people that would be driving through Denton going someplace else. Somehow or another they got word that they could stop at the church that's when we was on Boliver. We gave food out and gave clothing and stuff. Sometimes they would be people that would just be driving through.

Chapter Five

I remember one couple, they was just driving through and someone told them that they could get help, you know with food. They didn't have money enough to do their laundry. So, while they went to find a job, why I did their laundry. That was a blessing too, to do something for people. I had it down here where this one guy came in and he was driving through, and he had been in prison. He lived in Indiana I believe, but anyway he said he had a wife and two little girls at home. He stopped at the clothing room. We gave him everything that he had need of and even you know on the spiritual side. We prayed for him and he finally told us that he had cancer. He was the skinniest little ole thing you'd ever seen in your whole life. I think he was littler than Mike. But anyway, he was really sick. He had just gotten out of prison. He was ready to go home. He really was. We prayed with him and talked to him. While we was praying for him, why he fell out in the spirit. He shook his head and he didn't know what was going on. He said what's that, what was that? Mike told him well that was the Holy Spirit, the power of the Holy Spirit. He never had anything like that before. He was quite amazed at what had happened to him. We never saw him again and probably never will. I just know that the Lord touched his life and touched his heart that day. I felt like that he was healed. He acted like it and said well he didn't hurt anyplace. We took it that he was healed.

Then another little thing that uh…well I don't know whether it was little or not, it was pretty big to everybody. I'd take food over to Mike's apartment and I would cook. That's when we was having lunch with the pastor every Tuesday. When we first started, why maybe they'd be two, or three

Chapter Five

there, four, or something like that. They'd just bring a little sack lunch you know. One day I thought well, I think I'm gonna just cook a big meal. I fried chicken and I made gravy and I made biscuits and I made mashed potatoes and green beans and apple salad. Just a big, big meal. So I'd take all this stuff over to Mike's and I'd cook it over there and then take it over to the church. So finally, I think we had about half of the church that came for lunch. But anyway, I enjoyed it. I just enjoyed it so much to think that I could do something like that for people. I made quilts 'till I can't even remember how many I made. I made quilts for the nursery, I made Debbie and Randy a quilt and I made Mike a quilt. I just, everybody that come along I made a quilt for them. Of course, them days are over. The nursery I had a lot of, uh, I made a lot of quilts for there. Then I'd take these double matt pants that I would get and they didn't seem like that anybody wanted to wear at that time, they were real heavy. So I would cut them up and then I would make quilts for the orphanage. I remember one time too, I had a great big box full of stuff that I would send to the orphanage I just put it out in the back of the church there and I told everybody what to put in it. Toothbrush, toothpaste, combs and socks, whatever they wanted to do you know, put in that box. When we got ready to send the box, it was full. It was a great big box. I used to make quilts for the orphanage out of these pants.

The next thing I could think about was my book. One morning the Lord woke me up about oh, I would say around 3 o'clock or something like that. I was so wide awake. So, I guess the Lord wanted me to be real awake so he could tell

Chapter Five

me what he wanted. He told me he said *write a book*. I stood there about half dazed. You know I sat there on the bed and that's all he said was *write a book*. 'Course I went to complaining and said well Lord, I can't write a book. I don't have an education; I don't even know how to spell or anything. I can't do this, or I can't do that. I was complaining. It was a wonder he hadn't knocked me over for complaining. Anyway, that's what He told me, and he told me three times, he said *write a book*. Well, the third time that he told me, why I began to know that it was the Lord speaking to me, I knew I better shape up and do what he told me to do. So, I said well Lord, if you want me to write this book, your gonna have to help me. You're going to have to completely do it because I don't know the first thing about writing books. Or I don't know anything about what to do. He didn't say anymore but just three times, he told me *'write a book'*. Well, the last time he told me, I began to get a little excited about it you know. So, Mike came over to get me to go to work. I told him about it, well he was a little bit excited, but not too much. Anyway, the next morning the Lord woke me up at the same time and he told me what the title of my book was to be. It was *"Step Out Into the Sunshine."* At that time I didn't know what he meant about that and I didn't know why that he gave me that title. I couldn't have come up with that title. But he said *"Step Out Into the Sunshine"* that was what the title of the book was gonna be. Well that got me really excited. 'Cause I knew that nobody in this wide world would have thought about a title like that, but God. I told Mike about it and we both began to get excited about it. The next morning, he told me at the same time, he told me what the color was going to be. What it was going to look like. It was going to

Chapter Five

be a book about as big as this page. Right down from one corner to the other...up here was just a golden sunshine color. Down hear on this half was just black, as black as coal. Then the title of the book was gonna be right across here. It wasn't 'till, oh, I don't know several months after that, that I knew why he gave me that title. Because even though I had been a Christian a long time and had the baptism of the Holy Spirit and everything, but they was a lot of things I was in the dark about. I didn't know, didn't understand. I hadn't had my heart opened up for something to see the real joy of life. And I didn't have that peace you know that I should have. I finally began to put two and two together and found out that that's why God told me that, *Step Out Into the Sunshine*. I was way back here in the shadows, in the dark about a lot of things when I began to see all because of Randy's teachings. He was the one that helped me through to see what I just didn't understand. I praise the Lord for that title to that book. And this book, the front of it was gonna be sunshine and darkness. Well he wanted me to just get out of that darkness and into the sunshine. It was real neat.

Then I guess they was a, well, this may not be in order, well right after that, but anyway, when I had the heart attack at the church, why I went into the hospital and I was in there a week and then they took me to Dallas to Medical City or something. So, I guess I was pretty well gone because the doctor said that one of my arteries was closed to 95% and that's pretty much. And I had another one that was closed 65%. They said I had to have surgery. So, I went into surgery about seven o'clock in the morning. The surgery went fine and everything, but one of the arteries burst and I lost four

Chapter Five

pints of blood. I was just really, just on the verge of going. But I knew what was going on. Whenever they was doing surgery and they put me out, the Lord spoke to me and I asked the Lord, why am I suffering so much. He told me well, then he took me back to the cross and he showed me how he had died and poured out his blood for me and just really had a lot of pain and everything. He Just told me all this and he took me back to the cross and showed me how he had to suffer for me. So, I said well Lord, if you have a purpose in this well, I'll suffer anything for you. Oh! When that artery burst, it was just like somebody, well they said that three doctors was just pressing on that to keep it from bleeding anymore. It just felt like a 500-pound weight on me. They said well they almost put 500 pounds of weight on me to kind of keep that from uh… Then they had to go do surgery on that and close that all up and clean it out and everything. We'll I was pretty sick. I was in the ICU from the time I went in for surgery, when they did the surgery and took me into the ICU, I was in there until way in the night. Well I don't know, seven or eight o'clock at night I believe it was. I knew I was pretty bad.

My daughter stayed right there with me. They didn't even give her a pillow or anything. She laid down on that concrete floor to rest a little bit. She couldn't stand there all the time. She stood there, for I don't know for how long. So finally, I told her I said well, I think you better call Randy. She went and called Randy and it wasn't very long before Randy and Mike was there. Mike Wallace. They came in and they had a monitor up there where they could see me, but we couldn't see them, the nurses. Well Randy looked up there and said,

Chapter Five

"God is still on the throne." Telling them that, you know, God is still on the throne, we're just gonna go through this. So, he came in and he said, "Well Harriet I guess the ole devil's got ya now." I was just so sick that I just didn't hardly know where I was and everything, but I just opened my eyes a little bit and I'd go, "Uh, uh! He's not gonna get me." I was just so weak you know, I was just about dead. He said, "Yeah, the ole devil, he's really got you this time." I said, "Uh uh, he's not gonna get me." They started to prayin' for me and don't you know that from then on I started getting better. I think I was in ICU for about four days.

When they took me up to my room, it was kind of a ward like where they was six beds. Every woman that was in there had the same thing I did, the very same thing and they was just taking their turn having surgery. About I don't know how long it was, I don't think it was very long, I had been in ICU four days. So, I thought I was getting pretty good. I felt pretty good. So, one night, I was talking to all these ladies. About the time I hit the bed I was talking about the Lord. They was three saved, three women saved and two of, that I know of, that was healed. So, one night after supper, why I got up out of that bed and I had tubes all over me and the machine I had to pull along and everything. I went over to this other lady's bed. We had been talking back and forth, she was pretty close to my bed. Pretty soon I just got up and I went over there and started talking to her and praying with her and what have you. And it just seemed like the words just rolled out of my mouth. I didn't even have to think about what I was gonna to say. I just told her. Well, she wasn't saved. She was saved there and then she was healed. She was

Chapter Five

supposed to go down the next morning to have surgery. When they took her down why in about an hour, they took her back. They didn't have to do surgery on her. She was completely healed. I tell you, the joy that went over me, I just was so happy. Of course, I didn't do it. The Lord was the healer. He permitted me to talk to her and pray for her. Anyway, the nurse had come in and she had seen me standing up over there. I think I was there about 2 hours. They come in to put us to bed and I was still standing there. She come and went out and waited a little while and then pretty soon she'd come back and I was still standing there and talking to her and praying and everything. I didn't care how loud I was gettin', I probably was. Anyway, she finally had to come over to her bed and get me. She said, Harriet, you've just got to go to bed. You're not supposed to be up like this. I said well I've got something I had to do, I just had to get up out of the bed and go over there. This lady the next morning when she went down and they brought her back, she told me, she said would you do something for me?...Maybe it was at night before they brought her to surgery. She had two boys. She said, I'm going to give you their name, and their address and phone number. If I don't make it, why you tell them that I'm right with the Lord. That made me feel good too. I told her I would do it. But when they took her down for surgery and brought her back why she was alright. She was as happy as anybody I'd ever seen. Why I don't know her life, but she acted like she was just pretty wild. If that's the word I can say. It was wonderful how God used my life even on my death bed to pray for this lady and she was saved and healed. I'll always hold that in my

Chapter Five

heart that God just simply used me right there to do his work.

Then another time I had this kind of, well, I don't know if you'd call it a vision or what, but I call it a vision. I woke up in the night and they was the Lord showing me eagles. There were wings that were just covered down over me and just tucking their wings right under me and covering me completely to protect me. I thought well, the Lord was trying to protect me from something. I didn't know what it was, but anyway that eagles' wings were tucked under me like a hen does with her little chicks. Just puts them under her wings and protects them from any storm. I can remember one time when they was a bad tornado and this hen was on the porch in a box. The little chicks was all hatched out and everything and this tornado killed the hen and the chicks were all under this hen still alive. So, it felt like the Lord was protecting me from something. I was just thinking about myself; I wasn't thinking about anybody else. I had this urge to pray for Sharon and I was so burdened for her. I just laid there and I prayed for her and I asked the Lord was there anything going on with her, was she sick or something happened to her? I just felt this urge to pray for her real strong. I can't remember what happened from then. But anyway, when I got over to the clothing room, along about noon somebody had come after me to go to the hospital. My granddaughter had been in a terrible accident. I began to kind of put that all together. I know they was something about Sharon and something about protection and all this kind of stuff. Bonnie had five girls in a little truck (a Ford Ranger). It had had the cab on the back of it. Some of these

Chapter Five

girls was back there and when she turned, well, she hadn't been driving too long, when she turned the corner onto a gravel road, the truck had turned over. Threw them all out. They was all away from the truck and everything. Nobody got seriously hurt, but Bonnie got her head cut, oh about this much. I begin to put one and two together. That was what the Lord was telling me. Something about protection. He had protected them girls. That was kind of a warning I guess that the Lord had given me.

And I've been healed so many times that I can't even tell you, I can't remember. I was healed, well I don't know what was wrong, they was something wrong with my stomach. But anyway, one night I just saw a ray of light coming from up, out of space. That ray of light came down and just hit me right in the place that I was hurting. Afterwards it just went away, and I didn't have any more problems. And of course, there is a big story to that too. I went to the hospital and I forgot my papers, my orders what I was supposed to do. I guess the Lord was in that. He was just wanting me to be healed or he wanted to heal instead of havin' to go to the hospital and do all this kind of stuff. While I was living in Illinois, I ran my hand through a ringer. Washer, you know I had a washer that had a ringer on it. My hair got caught in the ringer and I reached up to get my hair out of the ringer. My hand just went right through the ringer. I had to take this hand and reach way over like this to turn the ringer off and it just pulled all my hair out of the front. This hand was just as flat as...just flat, flat. I went to the doctor. He said well, you don't have anything broken. Your bones in your hand is just crushed. 'Cause it is all crushed and all up here

Chapter Five

they was just big blood blisters. The blood had pushed all of it up there. It was a mess; it was just oh my. It was just finally beginning to kind of get blood and everything running down my hand. That was on Saturday. Sunday, I went to church. They prayed for me and I was supposed to go back to the doctor on a Monday. So, I went to the doctor on Monday. I went on Saturday and then on Sunday they prayed for me. I went back Monday morning to the doctor, and he said well there isn't anything wrong with your hand. I could just use it as good as I do now. There that hand, the bones was just crushed in it, but God healed me. It has just been one thing right after another that the Lord healed me from.

I fell out of a station wagon one time on a gravel road. Went down the little ditch like, and my head was about this far from the back wheel. Just way under the wheel about that far. If he didn't stop when he did, it would of about cut my head off. I had everything broken about me that I could think of. My shoulder was out of place. My collar bone was broken. I had five or six ribs broken, I had three blood clots on my head. Well, I know this is not the right way to say it, but it was my tailbone. My tailbone was crushed. They had to take four inches off of my tailbone. I was paralyzed about six months before they did that, before they took that off. This whole side, from my shoulder and my arm, and my side and my leg, it just took the meat, just took the hide and all off. It was just in awful shape. Clear down one side. I had a coat on that probably somebody gave me. It just tore it all up. Made rags out of it. About six months they did this surgery on this tailbone and then I had to learn to walk all

Chapter Five

over again. I just couldn't walk. I remember we lived on this farm. I went to stay with my mother-in-law in town and the doctor made me walk up and down this sidewalk. I was all bent over like that. He said well, whenever I walk try to straighten up a little at a time. About a year after that, why I got to where I could walk pretty good. Well, I never did get over it, but it was a very bad thing. One time I was down here. Sharon and Bill lived down here. I stayed quite a while with them. I got burned with hot grease. I gutted the kitchen out and the attached garage. It's a long story too, but I put this grease on the stove to melt. I was going to save it cause it looked like it was good to use again. I was always such a saving person that I just thought well, I'll save it. I put that grease on the stove and turned the stove on and walked through the hall. I didn't walk near as far as from here to that door. That grease caught fire and the whole kitchen burned out. Well I went in there and I picked up the skillet. Well first thing I did, I poured a cup of water in it...the worst thing you can do. So I picked up that skillet and I threw it out in the garage. She had a chair and a braided rug and everything and it burned all that up. So I lived about 5 minutes from the fire station. I took infection in my big toe which was burned and my thumb was swollen. I just barely got over that and then took kidney infection and had to go back to the hospital about three weeks.

Then they told me that this artery that had been closed up 65% it was about three years or something like that. They said surely it's clogged really bad now. I went to the doctor just for a checkup and she was just closing and we was just the last ones in there and we just barely got out the door and

Chapter Five

I had a heart attack. It just floored me. I just fell. It was the worst pain I ever had in my life. So Sharon took me back into the doctor and she took a cardiogram or whatever and she said I'm going to take you to the ICU. You've had a heart attack. They had to go and do a catheterization to the heart on that valve to see where it was clogged. I told them, you just do whatever you have to do. You won't find any clogging in there. Sharon and I had just almost been on our face praying you know that the Lord would just intervene for me and take that clogging out. So they took me to surgery and then they brought me back to ICU and three doctors came in. What I was telling these doctors before they took me in, I said you just wait and see, there is not gonna be any clogging. I serve a great big God and he can do anything. When they came back in, when they brought me out of surgery why they said well Harriet, there is not a bit of clogging in there. It's just as open and as clear as it can be. So there was another healing and that's just half of it. I tell you, I cannot tell you all of the healings that I have had and of course the hernia surgery I had this past year, that was pretty bad and the doctors didn't think I was gonna live. I did, I fooled them. I told them I'm gonna live. So I came out of that. Then I broke my shoulder. It was pretty bad but then I got over that. Then I fell on the microphone stand over there at church when I was praying for somebody else. Bruised my spine. They said it was a lot worse than a break. If I had broke it why it wouldn't have been near as bad. I spent I don't know how many months with that, but the Lord brought me out of that and it just finally one day just went away. I didn't have any more pain or anything. Then when I first moved down here, I went over to Liberty, they

Chapter Five

was having church over there, Gary Adams (Pastor), and I was sitting in church one day and my heart just stopped. It just completely stopped. The Lord showed me my mansion. It was something that I just can not tell you. I just can't tell you what it looked like. It was just so awesome. I couldn't even tell anybody what happened after. I guess it must have stopped for just a few seconds or something like that, but it just absolutely stopped. I wasn't able to tell anybody. They was a lady sitting right by me. I wasn't even able to tell her what happened. So finally, I got to where I could tell her to get Sharon who was right back of me. There was two or three or four or something like that came up there and they just started praying for me. I still couldn't tell anybody what had happened to me. When we got home, I was able to tell Sharon that my heart had stopped and I was weak as could be. I guess I kind of had a heart attack then. Well, I got over that.

Anyway, the Lord had showed me my mansion and it was just the most beautiful thing I've ever seen in my life. I can't explain how beautiful it was. Then one day I was feeling like Lord, I just don't do anything. I'm just not doing anything for you and I felt so bad. Like I was just not of use for anything.

[Her vision] I wish I was an artist to paint the picture that he gave me. I saw this storm was raging over the sea. The waves were rolling high. The trees were almost flattened to the ground on the shore and the black clouds were gathering, just rolling black clouds. I looked over to some rocks out in the water. Not too far out from the shore. There these big rocks was. In the crevice of these rocks was a little brown bird.

Chapter Five

It must have been a sparrow. He was sitting there in his nest in the crevice of this rock and he had his head tucked under his wing asleep. The storm began to break and it went away. God told me now that is peace. He was referring to this little bird that was asleep on the nest during all this turmoil. He said now that is peace. I took him at his word.

It made me fill up with his peace and his love. John 16:33 tells about the peace of God. I can't remember just what it says, but anyway the Lord was telling me now that is the kind of peace that you want. That is the kind of peace that you have to have. From that day on, and that's been quite a few years ago (in '87) I've had this deep, I mean deep, settled peace that just overwhelms me. When I think about how he came down and filled me with that peace and love, He showed me that I was to be emptied out. Everything emptied out. Then he took this big vase and just slipped it right down inside of me and started to filling it up with his peace and it began to flow over. It just kept boiling over. Then he said you're like a sponge that is full of water or whatever, or oil. Oil is the thing that he told me. It was like a sponge full of oil and wherever you walk that oil will be dripping behind you and that oil of the Holy Spirit will be flowing over everybody else. I tell you it's a wonderful feeling. It still is. It's never left me. I've had that peace, that joy way down deep inside. I always say whether all the kings horses and all the kings men, they cannot pull it out. They cannot get that out of there. It doesn't make any difference what happens, what the devil tries to do to me. It's there to stay. It's way down deep inside, there is nothing that is gonna take it out. That's what happened to me and I still have that peace.

Chapter Five

Thank the Lord that I still feel that contentment. That real peace down in my heart. Then I had that stroke at church. Everybody started to praying and the ambulance came after me and took me over there. I don't know what time it was in the morning, but it wasn't even hardly through the start of the worship service 'till I got sick and they started praying for me. They took me to the hospital. It must have been around quarter 'till eleven I think it was. Anyway I got to the hospital and they did all kinds of tests, MRI and all this other tests that they take. At 2:30 that afternoon, why I sat up on the bed and I said, well I feel alright. I think I can go home now. Well the doctors wouldn't even begin to listen to that. They wasn't about to send me home whether I felt good or not. I was alright and then whenever they got the test back and the MRI and they put them things on my head and all that kind of stuff they take for a stroke. Why they came in and said, we can't find a thing. They is not a thing wrong. There again, the Lord healed me. I never had any kind of affects over it. I was just completely well. So that was another healing. Another little thing here, I don't have much time here. I don't think I'm gonna read about that.

The last thing that I want to tell you about is the vision I had of here…this place. I had so much to chuck full into this time that I can't get it all in. Anyway, this one morning, it seemed like the Lord always works with me in the morning. Maybe he thinks I'll be fresh. I woke up. He just woke me up to wide awake and alert. He just sort of, well, I call it a vision. I don't know what anybody would call it. I'll read this too because I can't remember everything that happened.

Chapter Five

"God woke me up one morning at the early hour. He took me to this New Creation Bible School. You know how Paul and several different people in the Bible tell about how they was just carried away in the Spirit. Well, that's what I was. It was just the Spirit. I was carried over here to this place (New Creation Bible School – UNT Campus Denton, TX). Well, I was up there on the stage. When I was carried over here, I was on Angel's wings. The Spirit was just so rich. I walked up the path to the door and he said take off your shoes, this is Holy ground and the Holy Spirit was all around me. There were people lined up to get in. It was that door. They was just way down there. It was just in a straight line and waiting to get in that back door. The Lord said that whoever comes in this place will never be the same. Whenever you enter in that door you're not going to be the same. He said this was a learning place, a school and a college where you learn and it was just really gonna be from the very, like the primary, beginners in school and work up until you went to college and you would learn. To be a learning place and I think you found that out here. A learning place. I've never been in anyone of the classes or anything. The Lord gave me four words. Saneko Senoko Sonoko Sinoko. I said Lord, what does this mean? What do these words mean? He didn't tell me, but it just seemed like the Holy Spirit just started telling me what they meant. He said it was going to be the different races, the different languages and the different nationalities that anybody, it didn't make any difference what they were. Just different nationalities and languages and everything that would come into this school. Nobody would be put out. Everybody would be accepted. After they got in this place, they'd never be the same again. They would be completely different people when they went through this school. They would be taught God's word and they would really learn. Then he took me to the upper room and I can remember the very second that he did that. Not just upstairs but he took me into that upper room. Like the day of the Pentecost, and there the Angels were singing

Chapter Five

and people were talking in different languages and they were praising God. It was just like, well I guess on the day of Pentecost. It was really something. I heard singing and praising and rejoicing and I was just overwhelmed by His presence. He told me, He said to pray without ceasing."

I had the urge to have a prayer meeting in my home. It has been three or four years now, but we have had prayer meetings in my home every Thursday, and we've seen so many people that was healed and saved and everything else. We even prayed for our cats one time. One lady at 9:30 at night came to my house and she said do you pray for cats? Well, I said I know that the Lord loves cats, animals and dogs and whatever. I know that he loves them and he has them there for a purpose. I said, sure I'll pray for her. She had taken her little cat to the vet and it was real sick and it was just about dead. So that night she came to me to pray for it. She went and got it the next morning and there wasn't anything wrong with it. It was just as alive and happy as it could be. We always laugh about praying for the cat. It doesn't make any difference. We can pray for animals, cats, and dogs, and whatever. We prayed for just about everything under the sun. People came with some of the weirdest things for you to pray for. I thought well, God loves that person and He'll answer the prayer. Well, so that's I guess the end of my story. There is a little song that says 'This is my story'.

This is my story, this is my song,
Praising my savior, all the day long.
This is my story, this is my song,
Praising the savior, all the day long.

Chapter Five

I don't even know how to thank all you people. I love you, every one of you. I have a place in my heart for every one of you. One's not any better than the other. I have such love for each one of you. I just thank you and praise you for praying for me so much and for holding me up. You've been so good to me. I just thank you from the bottom of my heart. And I thank the Lord that he has always been with me. He stays with me every step of the way. I'm so glad that I know him today. And Randy has been a great support to me to come to the place where I really know him. I knew Jesus. I knew him as my Savior and I knew him as my healer, but I didn't know "Him" and that's what I always say that this banner...it wasn't a banner, but what was on the Boliver wall (Church on Boliver St, Denton TX) it said 'Come to know Him, then go out to show Him'. That's been my motto. I wanted to know Him. I didn't want to just know about him, I wanted to *know* him. I still want to learn and I still want to know more and more all the time. I learn everyday. I praise the Lord and thank him all my life even though it has been a pretty rough life. I just thank Him that He's helped me through each thing that I had to go through. I know that he is with me and He'll never leave me. I'm ready and it doesn't make any difference. I don't know how much longer I'm gonna be here on earth, but whenever, He'll keep me here until He says it's enough. Whenever he does, I'm bound for Heaven. I'm not afraid to go because there is so much to gain and so little to lose. I just feel like I'll be gaining an awful lot when He takes me home. I just want to be what he wants me to be while I'm here. I hope that you've gotten something out of this. Why, when I first started, it didn't matter whether anybody got anything out of it or not.

Chapter Five

It done me good. I obeyed Him because that's what He told me to do. I hope you've gotten a little something out of it and I love y'all, every one of you, I love you so much.

"There was about a half a bushel left that I didn't get in."

Chapter Six
A Tribute to Harriet Hankla

April 28, 1990

The following are excerpts from a video of Harriet Hankla's 75th birthday party.

Harriet's Story of the Airplane 1984
Well I got on this, what I thought I was getting on was a plane. I was coming down here *(to Texas in 1984)* and was at the St. Louis Airport. My friend (Ralph Shook) had brought me to the airport. They was redoing the airport and fixing it all up. So they really had everything all pulled up. So they got ready to load us on the plane, which I thought I was getting on the plane. I went and got out of the terminal and stepped right out onto the plane, which I thought was the plane. I was looking for my seat number. My seat number was 4A. I was looking all around you know and I thought well surely it would be right when I first went in. I said to this guy "I can't seem to find my seat number." He said "Well, just sit down anyplace." I said "Well I'll sit right here if it's all right." He said: "Yeah it's all right." I sat down on the seat and I began to look for my seat belt. Well I looked on each side of me and I felt for my seat belt and I didn't see any seat belt and I looked to see if anybody else had any seat belt on. Everybody begin to look at me like if I was kinda coo coo you know and I guess I kinda looked like it. I looked

Chapter Six

all around. On the left side of the plane, or I thought was a plane was a great big row and in the middle, I was in the middle section. It looked awful long to me, I thought well what kind of a plane is this? It looks like a sky rocket or something. I said I don't think I want to go up in this plane. Pretty soon, I looked around and I told this guy, "I don't think I've ever been on a plane like this." If I hadn't said that I'd been alright. I messed myself all up. Everybody sat there so silent like. They never said a word. This great big lady sitting right across from me, she looked at me like "boy I tell you what...I never in all of my life." Everybody just never even cracked a smile. They just looked so solemn; you could of herd a pin drop. They never said a word or nobody moved. Nobody even laughed, it wasn't even funny to them 'cause I said I had never been on a plane like this before. The plane begin to come down. It was on one of these hydraulic things you know and slowly come down making this shhhhh sound. It began to come down and I didn't think anything about it. It backed up you know and got down to the ground and backed up and it started whirling and it just dawned on me that I was on the shuttle bus. When I got to the airport and I met Sharon and Bill, I was laughing so hard, I couldn't even tell them what happened. I was just rolling and laughing. The shuttle bus had rolled right up close to the plane. We offloaded the bus and right onto the plane. This great big lady had set right across from me again on that plane. It was about halfway home that I got to the place where I could tell them what was going on. I was laughing so hard I was almost sick. Ralph had told me that now whenever you get there why you call me collect and let me know that you got down there alright. Whenever we got

Chapter Six

there, why I said I'm supposed to call Ralph and let him know that I got down here alright. So I went to the phone and I called him. When he picked up the phone, he started laughing. I know what was going through your mind all the time, he said, but I couldn't warn you. He said he could see me, but I couldn't see him. He said, "I couldn't warn you, I couldn't tell you what was happing." He knew what was going through my mind. I didn't know. He knew I thought that I was on the plane. Then we just sit there and started to laugh. We couldn't talk to one another because of the laughing.

Ruth Williamson – (Friend from Church)
Harriet, I have a scripture that really bless us and I just want to remind you of it. Now, she knows, and we all know that when you are in Christ Jesus, we all have His righteousness. So we can say that Harriet is righteous and we'll be saying the truth. Somewhere along Psalm 92 about verse 12, the word says the righteous shall flourish like a palm tree. They shall grow like cedars in Lebanon. Planted in the house of the Lord, they shall flourish in the courts of our God, and they shall still bear fruit in old age and they shall stay fresh and green. Another one that is our favorite, Psalm 103, Harriet has learned how to bless the Lord, and she blesses the Lord with all her soul and all that is within her blesses the Lord. She didn't forget His benefits. She remembers that he forgives all her sins and heals all her diseases and he rescues her from the pit and crowns her with love and compassion. He satisfies her desires with good things so that her youth is renewed.

Chapter Six

Jim Vetter
Apr 28, 1990

"A son's tribute"
I'm grateful to God that I can say these words of thanks to my mother while she's still alive and well. More often than not we've neglected until it is too late, and then delivered with great remorse at the funeral. Mother at this celebration of your 75th birthday, I'm sure your memory is better than mine, but I'll reflect on some of those incidents that make you very special to me. I remember you as you prayed. I don't know if you realize it, but it made a lasting impression on me to come to the house and watch you pray. I was just a little guy. Not many people know that you were preaching. I remember how proud I was when you spoke at that interdenominational meeting at Batch Town. I wrote down Batch Town, I think it was Batch Town. Boy I tell you, that was first class. I don't remember what you spoke on but you've got to realize, I was probably 12 at the time. We had these interdenominational meetings about once a month or so and another such meeting the pastor got up and he made this long appeal for an offering for some really good cause. If you knew what this cause was for, you'd be happy to donate. And then when the money was given, he gave the money to mom for new glasses. She wasn't gonna get new glasses otherwise. Mom I remember you as a survivor. You made do with very little. Creating feed sacks and flour sacks and got enough of the same print for a dress that became a social event. Remember when you cooked a mud hen for us after we were trying to recuperate from the flu and we were so hungry and we didn't have anything to eat. Do you all

Chapter Six

know what a mud hen is? It's a loon. I don't know if that thing ever got tender but it tasted alright. Remember that old one lung Maytag washing machine that seemed to be a luxury?...How that thing smelled, but we had enough food because you canned everything in sight. Folks you just can't feel the pride when you remember how good that canned beef tasted. I was reminded about a few years back when I got a hold of some canned beef from a Mormon store house. It was very similar. Mom sometimes you did have a little something of yourself that you always gave away. I remember one occasion when you were ill at home. The rest of us went off to grandma's house for dinner. They sent you some chicken and some pie. Then a bum showed up at your door and he ended up eating your dinner on the porch. I remember it well and I was five then. Another occasion it was plums. There must have been two bums at that house. You were the brightest jewels in your crown as your roll as a devoted wife. You truly lived for your husband and thrived on your relationship. There were occasions when most women would have hired a lawyer. Remember being forced to cook for 22 coon hounds? Remember living for years without an outhouse or an in-house? The nearby barn was a very poor subject. And we won't even talk about all the water gravy and water biscuits. You were at your very best during Kenny's long illness, serving his needs around the clock with an act of love and great devotion. From a very difficult family situation, to early marriage and having to raise your family in poverty, to the loss of three husbands and more illness than anyone should have to face, you emerged as a choice servant of God. You've come a long way.

Chapter Six

Randy Nusbaum – Pastor of New Creation Church – Denton, Texas
April 28, 1990

We have a wonderful relationship and it is in the Lord. When you're in the ministry there is times where you are down and out and a lot of people don't know when you're going through something hard. Harriet seems to know. By the Lord, she would always right a note. She still does this to this day. Just at the right time it would be the sweetest note to me about just encouraging me in the Lord. It has just kept me going many times when I needed to hear from a human being that thought it was worth me keeping on. Her life has been just one great example, not just to me but to everyone in the church of what Christianity is all about. I've had so many young people come up to me, some in tears, talking about Harriet how the words that she spoke or just her presence, just the glow that she has, has kept them going. It has really ministered to them. About a month ago, she tried to check out on us early. So she was there in the hospital, it was late at night. Sharon called me concerned that she was gonna go on to be with Jesus. Harriet passed the word on that she wanted me there. So, Mike and I hopped in the van, we drove down and walked in that room and it didn't look too good. Sharon didn't look to good either. But Harriet has got this thing where I don't care what's going wrong, if she thinks the Devil is getting the best of her, she gets mad. She was barely hanging. I prayed for her, and there wasn't any response from her, so I said, well, I guess Harriet the Devil's gonna win this one. And she said "What" I said, yeah, it looks like you're gonna lose out on

Chapter Six

this one. I don't guess Jesus is on the throne this time. She said "What!" Every time I said something, she'd get a little stronger. Well, we had to go downstairs, Sharon and I and Mike, we had to leave the room so they could change the sheets. When we got back she was preaching to the nurses. I mean she had the Devil on the run. To be honest with you, Harriet has been like a mother to me and one of the strongest supporters that I've had over the last couple of years, personally. For that I will be eternally grateful. I know in her heart and I'm sure that she would want me to say these words. If there is anybody that doesn't know Jesus as their Lord and Savior you need to see her. Because this woman here has lived it and proved it that Jesus is worth all. Spirit, Soul and body, she is a living example of the way to do it. If you don't know the Lord, and you want to know Jesus the way this woman does then if you're interested and you really want to get a good dose, say something to her.

Timothy David Malmer – Grandson
June 14, 2008

Most of my early childhood, Grandma Hankla lived far away and we would only have an occasional visit from her or we would take a family trip to Illinois to visit her and aunts and uncles. One year we took a trip to Illinois where I remember a big stump in the back yard of Aunt Norma's house that we would struggle to climb up on. At the time it seemed like a giant redwood tree, but as a small child it might not have amounted to more than an average tree stump cut off at four feet high. I remember getting my picture taken with everyone around that stump. I'm not sure why that trip was

Chapter Six

memorable to me but it may have had something to do with the fact that I was jealous over my younger sister Bonnie getting to stay the night at Grandma's house while the rest of us stayed at Aunt Norma's. I also got very sick, tossing my cookies all over Aunt Norma's front porch. We traveled all that way from Texas to Illinois in an old blue Ford sedan with the windows down. There were four of us kids crammed in the back seat. It must have been a twelve to fourteen hour drive with the usual "Are we there yet?" or "He's looking at me! She's touching me! Tell him to stop!"

Grandma was always very kind and never failed to have a little toy for us. During that visit, Grandma took us over to the house of her friend, Ralph Shook. I can still picture every detail of the outside of the house and his orchard I ran around. I liked Ralph a lot because he gave me a Bluebird house kit to build. This may have been a small token for him to give, but is one of the very few gifts I received as a child that I remember today. He couldn't have known that I loved to build. It was my passion in life to hammer boards together.

One year, I had even asked for wood for my birthday. My dad went to a construction site and filled that powder blue Ford's trunk with scrap wood, another of the few birthday presents that was the best of my memory. I can still see the trunk lifting, revealing a pile of lumber cut in many triangular shapes and looked like a mound of gold to me. I don't know if it was grandma or influence from her kids, but when we went to Illinois, we went fishing for catfish on the river and Uncle Glen would always find a day to take us to an auction

Chapter Six

or estate sale. This was especially fun for me because we got to take our car on the ferry to cross the river.

Year after year, one of our highlights was getting a box of Christmas presents from Grandma. We could always count on it. I'm not sure why it was so exciting because we knew the presents would be something simple from the five and dime store. Regardless of how simple the presents were, all four of us kids would enjoy seeing that package arrive and adding it to the pile of presents under the Christmas tree.

In the early 70's, grandma came to stay with us for a while as mom and dad went to Hawaii for vacation. I was very young. Each morning when I woke up, I always went to the kitchen to help myself to cereal. Well, Grandma didn't like me climbing up on the cabinets to get it by myself. I didn't understand why she wouldn't let me climb because before she came, that's what I did. I got my own cereal. So, the following days and weeks she stayed with us, I began going into her room early in the morning nudging her shoulder to wake her saying; "Grandma, can you get me some sur-real?" as she would describe it and how she repeatedly told the story for the rest of her life. She would always tell me to go back to bed. Only one morning, I was awakened by panic and chaos. Apparently, she had a grease fire in the kitchen. I heard the commotion and got out of bed only to be snatched out of the hallway and carried across the street to our neighbors in my underwear. I remember being under one arm and my brother Billy under the other carried headfirst. I was so embarrassed to be carried across the street with no clothes on. I don't even remember who carried me. Later I learned that Grandma had suffered burns and our garage was burned. After the fire department left and we were allowed back in the house I remember the unique smell of chemicals in the garage which they used to put out the grease fire. There was a chair and a throw rug that were charred and burned. I think it took years for that smell to clear out of our garage.

I am fortunate to have had the opportunity to grow close to Grandma during the last twenty years of her life. In the early 1980's, she moved to Texas to live with us permanently. We lived on Bonnie Brae Street in an old white farmhouse that the wind blew right through. The A/C rarely worked in the summer and the butane bottle was very expensive to fill in the winter. Grandma moved her furniture into a finished garage while mom and dad lived in an upstairs garage addition. There was no room for Bonnie, so she had a bed set up in a stairwell breezeway between the house and the finished garage where Grandma lived. Grandma would invite us into her room for stories. Her room was warm because she had an electric heater. She loved to tell stories of her past and I was fascinated with them. I could sit and listen to her tell stories for hours.

Eventually, she got her own apartment near North Texas State University (UNT Today). She frequently had issues with wild neighbors and loud parties, so she managed to get another apartment on the other side of town in a retirement community. I always enjoyed helping her.

Chapter Six

Each time I visited her apartment, she would have a task for me like furniture to move or monkey grass to dig up from around her front porch. We both had a love for plants. One time I made a flower bed for her around her porch. Today, I still have one of her hanging basket plants. We both shared many interests. She was part of the Audubon Society which got me interested in bird watching. We share an interest in the outdoors and nature, gardening and canning. I would frequently call her to ask her questions about canning recipes. In her older years, she gave me many of her canning pots, pressure cookers and utensils.

Recently, I found a wild patch of blackberries along a park trail. It brought back memories of how Grandma would pick and preserve anything edible in nature. Within a few days, I was back at that blackberry patch picking a gallon of berries and ended up with more than ten jars of blackberry jam. Grandma would have been proud.

Grandma Hankla was first a servant of the Lord. She was devoted to God and everything she did in life was to serve Him and others. Her struggles through life, all too plenty of the Silent Generation, should serve as a reminder to us how blessed we are today. Baby Boomers, Generation X, Generation Y or also known as "The Me Generation" have struggles small in comparison. Her life teaches us how good things are today and to pray and trust in God and thank him for blessing us and providing for us.

Chapter Six

Granny,
Through struggles and pain, sunshine and rain,
you've learned more in life than one can obtain.
You're knowledge and virtue, gentle and kind,
given by the Spirit of the Lord,
with whom you dine.
A life so magnificent, glorious and divine,
no matter the challenge the Devil to resign.
Your prayer for others and intersession so rife,
not taking for granted, God's will for your life.
Obeying His word and the guidance you seek,
is example to us all, His gifts should we be meek.
Bended knees hands folded, I pray to the Lord,
please let me be half of this woman you've adored.

Tim Malmer, Grandson

Chapter Six

Chapter Six

Chapter Six

Step Out Into the Sunshine

Disclaimer & Copyright Information

The information contained in this book is not to be considered medical, physiological or psychiatric advice, nor is the content intended to offer a cure, a course of treatment or a substitute for medical assistance. Please consult your doctor or a medical professional for any medical matter(s) affecting you or someone else, including depression, addiction, suicide or other illnesses.

Most of the events, locales, and conversations have been recreated/recalled from memories, therefore, some dates and/or events might not be completely accurate. Any stories or situations resembling any other persons or similar events are merely coincidental. All content is considered original according to the author and any similar content should be considered a coincidence.

Although the author and publisher have made every effort to ensure that the information in this book was correct at press time, the author and publisher do not assume and hereby disclaim any liability to any party for any loss, damage, or disruption caused by errors or omissions, whether such errors or omissions result from negligence, accident, or any other cause.

Transcribed by
Tim Malmer, Harriet's Grandson

Edited and Published by
Bonnie Malmer Rodriguez,
Harriet's Granddaughter

Cover designed by
Mike Rodriguez,
Harriet's Grandson (married to Bonnie)

Cover illustration, book design, and production
Copyright © 2020 by Tribute Publishing LLC
www.TributePublishing.com

Step Out Into the Sunshine

Step Out Into the Sunshine

www.ingramcontent.com/pod-product-compliance
Lightning Source LLC
Chambersburg PA
CBHW021114080526
44587CB00010B/508